IN POETRY, PROSE AND SONG

IN POETRY, PROSE AND SONG

Mitchell Alexander Jackson

CITI OF
BOOKS

CITIOFBOOKS, INC.
3736 Eubank NE Suite A1
Albuquerque, NM 87111-3579
www.citiofbooks.com
Hotline: 1 (877) 389-2759
Fax: 1 (505) 930-7244

Ordering Information:
Quantity sales. Special discounts are available on quantity purchases by corporations, associations, and others. For details, contact the publisher at the address above.

Printed in the United States of America.

| ISBN-13: | Softcover | 979-8-89391-287-6 |
| | eBook | 979-8-89391-288-3 |

Library of Congress Control Number: 2024917361

To all creative unknowns

TABLE OF CONTENTS

PROSE

SONG

INTRODUCTION

In Poetry, Prose And Song favors three parts. It's interest is in the here and now with voices of concern of present day. It's interest is in U.S. America, her culture––and especially the Black U.S. citizenry. While the previous Administrations saved not one home, this present Administration (Obama) preoccupied itself with foreign affairs and satisfying undocumented immigrants and illegals––on U.S. shores and abroad. That left little politically expressed concerns for the U.S. America's one hundred twenty million citizens. The U.S. was thought of as a part of a larger unit–whether economically or culturally. Political rhetoric was no longer "My fellow American," but "America." And the saying: "the American people" was replaced. "People in America" became the mantra. The U.S. American individual was no longer held in the hearts of the Court nor the politician. As early as 2013 ninety million Americans were unemployed. People in America swelled to three hundred million. One hundred twenty million Americans were cast adrift in a sea of one hundred eight million immigrants and illegals. Even now American families are living in cars. And the everyday U.S. individual was left to his everyday life with its everyday concerns.

The three parts of *In Poetry, Prose And Song* favor the lives of the individual American, as each individual struggles to maintain sight of the American Dream.

POETRY

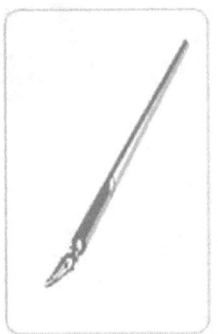

DARK AND SHINING GLORY

Dark and shining Glory from out Puritan's
Prompt grasp of encroachment
Wrenched you––bid you stand.

Look at your dark faces. Reflected in the glass
Are ferrules––dark, unmoving––
Etched there by the past

Can but the past so telling, to crease your lulled skull
Not stir you from your slumber?
Not brief you to your thrall?

Oh, how you chide: "I'm free. All men do clasp my
    hand!"
Yet hesitant, when doing so,
To free it once again.

Stir your heart from slumber; charge your mind alert.
Remember the past ever––
Pleasure, as well the hurt.

Awake unto the doing. Just counsel keep in sight:
Thus mark you fellow wrongs
As wrong is marked by right.

Dark and shining Glory––island lose to seas
Of mankind; in God's glory
Arise to victories.

APPETIZERS

I miss my chicken gizzard
and my chicken necks!
If I knew which store catered
—well, then what the heck!

No high gas registered
will sway me from my trek.
I love my chicken gizzard
and my chicken necks!

AWASH!

Pelting rain and torrent winds
Smash against cloak, cap—late
Wind-shot rivulets blown,
Winding down my nape.

Bracing on—an instant tossed;
I must fence off second thrust:
Step on step, to the bone
—Awash... beyond the husk.

Gaining force all over drains
Skies to stain cloudy gray;
I, near thrown kite-sky-borne
—hugging tight the day.

Blessed Shades Of Equality

"Historic Moment Unfolds
With Obama's Nomination"
—America's breath on hold,
Fanning congratulations!
Other historic feats
Placed Black souls on the street;
Perhaps, his is cause for celebration.

Headline of local paper
Greeted early the breaking dawn.
Is it the soul's deal-breaker,
Feigning not publicist's charm?
Eight years' historic acts

Fell hearts and souls to mat:
Ugly fueled warmth, sweet calm devastation!

An historic moment came—
The census was being counted!
The Black souls fell back in gains:
Straining Reagan ploys pounded!
Hour's *president* proclaimed
Homeless Black—count: *no gain!*
—*No increase*, disposed; Black remained hounded.

"President" of the hour
Sold Black eager souls on "first" homes;
Though all was in his power,
Grieving souls—consumed by loans
—Leaved in indebtedness

By that unrighteous kiss!
The climax: many stressed souls, and homes gone!

Then, there is *Katrina*!
—Devastation and no bounds.
As if served a subpoena,
Bulldozing hopes, all dreams—down!
And Black soul's dreams went dark;
Cries touched not his warm heart;
Edict bedded Black homeless to the ground.

The "icing" on the cake—
And by this fabled Christian land:
Without any real debate,
Disowning child, woman, and man
—Out! Onto the street, be blessed!
Homeless streets by Christmas!
Season's breath slays our God's redemptive plan!

Unfolds historic moment—
Now, is all in hesitation.
This nation's pores bleed of sweat;
Failing hearts question creation.
Years' passed historic feats
Did not race the heart's beat,
Why now doubts—these fears of tribulation?

BLESSINGS OR CURSES

Why all the noise in such a public place,
heaping upon that woman loathed disgrace!
The two-year-old would cry out "mental case!"
—Bleeding of the soul, you make spirit displaced.

What man are you, to bellow, bray and shock!
Notions of *royalty?* Or fleeting lark?
Show yourself to be Black man at the heart
—Color of the heart it is that sets apart.

Man of castle? Or are yo just a *fool*
Ruling poorly? She is not your tool;
For that *help meet* deserves the "golden rule."
Blessings or curses—wedded you which school?

Monstrous ravings produce more than her dread
Leading unto despised, unwanted bed;
When the heart is so vilely monstrous fed,
Festoons of hatred reigns! Shame's upon *your* head!

BLISSFUL MIND REPRIEVE

How comforting—blessed be
Torrent rains! Majestically
It overflows unto forgetting
Preying thoughts that spike at whetting!
Painful mind relieved! Blessed birth,
    Sweet peace, conceived!

Now, Blessed thing, conquer me;
Un-set trains of soul's own debris!
Arrows and slings—and past fretting
Left scabs and scales need shedding!
Blissful mind *reprieve!* Blessed birth,
    Sweet peace, relieve!

Boo-hooing Lost TV

I owned a good relation
With my Cathode ray:
My TV respected me,
'Til they took it away!

Not one day's shop service;
Not one fearful stall.
Then the regs sprouted legs
And took away my all!

BUT A BREATH

Gospel wails, longing, singed the blast
of *terrorist* winds—that harassed
soul and mind and spirit,
usurping, to un-wit
God's purpose on this side of the glass.

Low and long, next a broken pitch
characteristic assailed to stitch
torn and tattered pulse strains
worshiping—*sweet* refrains!
Winds confronted: for woes salve cathect!

But a breath, tone not lasting long:
sweet, refreshing air... and soon gone.
Yet the seed of hope: *planted*,
retiring fear borne dread,
as course winds bellow, pledging more harm!

BUT CLOUDED ROOMS

A rustling thought transpired to find
Its own across a tepid mind
—As distinct as the Georgia pine,
It thirsted to waken me.

It needled corridor at call;
It then bustled through languid halls
—And brushing yet the silent walls
With certain skilled industry.

The firstling was a thought without;
It soon filled in—creating doubt
—More whisper, now, lethe—at rout,
It kindled a memory.

A second thought picked up the thread;
My mind succumbed to being led:
No anxiety, no sense of dread
—What motive could this source be?

In eager mind—awake, at last
—Could I almost relive the mass!
The procession lately had passed;
She warmly smiled—most tenderly.

Her ginger touch would spark my hand
—The Eucharist now in demand,
Priest ministers of first his band
—His processional company.

But clouded rooms re-framed my mind;
My soul grievous: the *left behind*
Was akin to spirit supine
—Yet were locked with absent key.

CELL PHONE BANDIT

Too many thoughtless drivers
Won't leave risk alone.
The least, they're turning corners,
Manning their cell phone!
Down go the caution reflector poles!
Down go street signs and strung fence, too!
In jeopardy are pedestrian souls.
Nothing these bandits won't undo!

No glaring rays of midday,
Nor the moonless night
Would sway phone use towards caution,
Shearing cell delight.
Mad is logic of reflected care!
Mad is the mind that stirs such wit!
Let cost and value for maintenance flair
—Knowing the cost is the public's.

The monsoon rains have, too, seen
Reckless disregard.
Bridges can become victims:
Crashing's in the cards!
The hapless Cyprus can't hold its own!
Street pole, bus sign would need repairs!
Yet cell phone bandit, dazed on call, groans
—Hoping soul acts, "I'm out of here!"

The beautiful surroundings
Reveal tattered strains
Solely from cell phone musing,
Holding back new gains!
New finance for old abusive needs:
Needs *via* wiles of cell phones on display,
Reduce coffers with, "pretty, please?"
—Shearing needed programs—snuffed away!

CONTENDING SHADE

Off leaned this shaven tree; half itself cut away!
Reduced its greenery—resembling the paltry;
Meager in countenance: gone was half its wealth!

My thought: *What industry wilt to control,*
Lessen what could be—contemptuous overload!
It leaned in the summer sun, grace... half itself.

Off base contending shade must soothe the weary
    brawl;
As Creator bade—stripped of stately charm—the mile
Must it maintain; husbandman butchered, bled.

To leave it destitute to the season's plunder,
What mind doeth recruit—detract grand wonder!
—Cuffed wilt duty, shorn of limb and crowning head!

FELL CELEBRATION

—A Southern Memory—

Why is celebration always short-lived in America?
Remember that Kennedy? John—
Before coming to harm?
All eyes were glued to the tube.
Even that J. Edger Hoover was fooled.
       And Black souls celebrated.
       Celebrated!

And then his relation—brother, Bobby,
Likewise did suffer:
Two brothers; gone Innisfree; gone!
Too soon coming to harm.
Black cries wailed blue by that few
—Elvis idolized Hoover. Who knew!
       Black love fell—anticipated.
       Anticipated!

And The underrated incident of Rosa Parks—*kosher!*
When that Martin Caused to key the fond,
Embraced listing of arms—
Before coming to harm.
Filled eyes; ensued tears infused!
A thorn to G-man Hoover—removed.
       And Black joys dissipated.
       Dissipated!

FOUR EQUESTRIANS COURTING

Mrs. Barbara Waters—
> Saving our daughters;
> Mrs. Schwarzenegger, the same—

While their champions
Destroy fathers and brothers:
> Leaving mothers alone to grieve their pain.

To wait: up comes the new breeze
> Calming waves at ease.
> With cooler breezes blowing again—

Might we then begin
To see our Ms. Winfrey
> Beyond what her own talents had obtained.

Ms. Sibyl Shepard's anguish,
> Wailing in protest—
> bemoaned the fact that true loyalty

Came up short—dismissed
Heart's cry: that hope's not vanquished.
> Feeling denied, she voiced this misery.

GONE HOME TO GLORY

Conway Twitty

—Was a man of my heart.
Wore a pompadour—
The closest thing to mod.
    The night that he died,
    You know somebody cried!
            —A man the heart could adore!

Now he has...
    Gone on the road
            For the last time.
    Dropped his heavy load
            For the last time.

            —You know he's
            Gone home.
Yes, he's gone on
To glory!

                    ...

Johnny Cash
—Was a winner by choice.
He made it happen
With his guitar and voice.
    And his strident cry—
    My, how the time does fly!
            —His world you had to let in!

Now he has...
    Cried out his song
        For the last time.
    And he picked along
        For the last time.

      —You know he's
      Gone home.
Yes, he's gone on
To glory!

...

June Carter Cash
—Was a singer of style.
Remembered her roots:
All country the whole mile.
    He songs root to be
    Etched on in memory!
        —A soul who's from the "old school"!

Now she has...
    Sung out her song
        For the last time.
    She had us sing along
        For the last time.

    —You know *she's*
      Gone home.
Yes, she's gone on
To glory!

...

The country heart
—Is now grieving its lost:
Souls not forgotten;
Still silent tears, remorse.
　　Oh, when these lights died,
　　You know somebody cried!
　　　　—Three held as dear beloved friends!

Now they have...
　　Gone on the road
　　　　For the last time.
　　Sung us their song
　　　　For the last time.

　　—You know *they've*
　　　Gone home.
Yes, they've gone on
To glory!

HOPING THE BUS

Is it the bus?
I hope it's the bus—
Time doesn't rush!
It would be a plus!

My hair is all mussed
Since that last gust.
I hope it's the bus
For the rest of us!
...
Bus, come with care.
Now, don't you dare
Find needy repair,
With me sitting here!

My man may fear
I'm not sincere—
An hour's despair,
Yet I am still there!

...

Is it the bus?
I hope it's the bus!
Time doesn't rush
For the rest of us!

I'LL BE THERE

If I had a Charger
    All white, with long mane
    I'm there for you, baby
        —Altogether *and* sane!

If you were off behind
    The enemy line,
    Call on me, baby
        —I'll be there on time!

If out far—on Mars... even all the gods
Distempered and cruel
    Can't keep me
From you!

          ...

If now you sit mending
    Your heart with pledged thread,
    I'm there for you, baby
        —My love's being fed!

If they say it's a crime
    To speak your own mind,
    Call on me, baby
        —All will be just fine!

If out far—on Mars... know no iron bars,
Walls built won't diffuse,
    Won't keep me
From you!

IN THIS LAND OF PROMISE

In this land of promise, where I ought to field my
    dreams,
In this land of Promise of the wheatfields and the
    streams,
Some unnatural conquest took apart with design
    scheme
        My hope's joyousness
        —here, to bleed me at the seams!

The endangered species is remembered—safe from
    harm;
Man's companion species, *too*, claims value for alarm;
And test subject species also marshal up a storm;
        But my dream's in pieces
        —yet, hearts loving here grow warm!

Off to lands of mystery—out to other kingdoms,
Off in lands of mystery we speak of laws and freedoms;
All minds—bent on history—and all the woes to come,
        Here, consigned misery
        as my soul's own champion!

Country's flag and celebration do mark our love's joys;
Country's love and aspirations keep hearts well
    employed;
With ensuing desperation we muster our toys;
        I, in desolation
        —am still bled by native soil!

IN THOUGHT AND PRAYER

I forgot to drink my water.
I forgot to take my pill,
Forgot the things that I ought to
    Remember for my will.

I forgot to ring for shades
To be pulled the length just right.
And I forgot to curse nursemaid
    On her way out last night.

...

Now, let me try *and* remember
My poor relatives someday;
That one churched pathetic member,
    I most needs cast away!

And that dreadful certain other
Divesting all his reserve—
Let his go, indeed, asunder
    For lost that he incurred!

Let me see, there are my nieces—
And each with a new excuse:
A dead child always displeases;
    Pure matriarch abuse!

And, too, why am I to bother
With grand children on the cusp:
Had "mom" but tried one bit harder
    "Child" would be one of us!

No such bother with the locals
That do service for their pay:
Postman, butcher, baker—all *trolls!*
    Dispel these right away!

Ah, of course! The reverend good right
Is most worthy—to be sure.
These past years, *shopping* here each night
    Proved himself quite a bore!

Now, who's left to be considered?
With my fortune on the line:
Opportunity delivered—
    Grasp! Or be left behind!
Not the coiffeuse—she's too mouthy;
No modiste here rich made!
Nuisance both! First gossips loudly,
    Next refuses set trade!

Not the chauffeur, nor the grocer,
Nor that stiff chinned pharmacist;
Nor the lawyer—nor the doctor:
    His remedy's my curse!

No butler, barber, nor banker—
Money-changer's worst of all!
But before I see my maker...
    A draught—*where is my shawl!*

...

They think, since I've long grayed,
This mind has left the station;
So then, let my memory fade;
    "Pooh!" on my relations!

Likewise, such acquaintance
Who would know me for a bag;
If such fools seek deliverance,
    Then know, I won't be had!

                                        ...

Ah—an exhaustive run.
And now am I much content;
Do prayerfully, lord, I now come
    —Your servant, suppliant.

House Saint Peter at the Gate,
For I know *not* what the hour.
Lord, last request, please—no debate,
    A must: an angelic choir!

INQUIRY

Or you king for a day—
Or some such dismay?
Or are you tapioca pudding
—A surprising gooding!

Or you man—or you mouse;
Have you come to bless this house?
Are you richly employable
—Or just more grievous toil?

Is the moon still at bay
—Or *now* heart's at play?
And the sun—oh, can you so tell:
Horizon? Or still *hell!*

Yesterday dispelled me;
Have you now the key?
Are thoughts different from "the thinking,"
Or, again, just a king!

INTO MID-LIGHT

Red brick, white trim
from which they made their way,
She 'abling him
—They, at a steady sway.
Just two stone steps
And she... upon his arm;
The air sun-swept
Range with no alarm:
    Bell chimed into mid-light,
    Cathedral bell—wholesome, bright!

...

Foliage, sky, spire—
Beneath, the campanile.
Buttress aspire;
The bells' greeting swell.
Chasuble garbed
(Upon a grade of leaves),
Age: youth non-robbed
—And all he thus receives.
    Come they into mid-light
    To out-reach hands newly bright!

Moment's notion
Upon a concerned brow;
Love, devotion
Not absent of the now.
Unmasked question
Escapes his unworn face.

And of flesh, sin?
He pleads redeeming grace:
　　Pleading into mid-light,
　　Embracing souls—spirit bright!

MY HONEY BUG

Loving *all* my honey bug!
She's ever with the squeezes and hugs,
And too sweet—but she's all mine;
Our each moment is quality time!
And when we kiss...
My honey bug insists
Heaven does not come down to dine!

Missing her is lonely blues—
Like having heard of funeral news.
No *fun* heart can breathe that gall;
Any strained brow is too huge a haul—
Too great a sting
For honey-sweet loving!
—Living the "old man"—lost the lord!

Knowing the *Word* isn't bad;
Her longing for me outweighs—a tad!
So, I'm hers for her delight;
Lose of my bug's love is pitched bled night!
Embrace the lord—
Go, recall the Saint Paul;
Burning kiss fuels *my* appetite!

NO BEARD AND NO PENSION

Why don't that bus
Stop at my door!
Why don't they give
Change any more!
Why must you be
Three to forty-four?
   I ain't understanding these things!

...

Sir, you're all denial.
The modern bus has style.
Means for the disabled is addressed;
Babes attend a Mother's breast.
Bearded age has a reserved chair.
Next time you ride, sir, forbear!
   The wise man lets the answer ring.

...

But why not *at*
My door, I say?
What must I have
Exact for pay?
You only touched
Things I don't portray:
   Ain't got no beard, and need no tit!

...

But sir, you are, indeed,
Less concerned with seed.
Verily you're of a crucial age,
Shortly will you, too, turn that page.
Your argument a child would reject;
A sage would fault the architect.
   Sir, control the bray with the bit!

...

That's why I ask—
Why not my door?
Ain't got your class:
Seventy-so,
Chauffeur drives you
Everywhere you go!
   And I—all crippled, still like so.

...

Sir, note, your blessing's
At hand—embrace the thing.

...

No! You, kind sir
Don't understand.
You plum through life
Choosing what demands
   —Thins your children will never know!

NOTIONS OR TRUE DEVOTION

I could climb Mount Everest—
But why would the heavens care?
And I would feel quite blessed
If mountainous winds
Blow me *not* into oblivion!
But, if still here—
Why would the heavens care?

I could fill my life with wealth—
But why would the angel's sing?
I could place on the shelf
Soul's pity—and swear
No allegiance brand should I wear.
Would I this thing—
Why would the angels sing?

Should I speak but "grand design"—
Now, what would the Savior say?
If stripped of humane mind,
God, love, devotion
Are merely cool, parlor notions.
Do I as may—
What would the Savior say?

PAPA'S HEART

Half way in and half way out
Third-floor chambered and full of doubt:
Mother left with him an hour
A yellow bundle—*warmth and smiles!*

The world hammers. Pains. Scars!
But his treasure—beyond dramas
So tenderly tucked in gentle arms
Swearing safety—shall know no harm!

Now papa smiles into the folds!
One gurgle—two... and, *oh*, up rose
His heart! *Precious.* Yet no measure
May truly show such wondrous pleasure!

BEST FRIEND COLLIER

My best friend Collier ran for de lawyer
And I waited for de chief police man
Things looking up. It's clear cut—–
Take the boy and run him on in.
It was after one... we finally come.
De station was in de uproar
Good man dead, de words was say.
He ought to pay a hell lot more!

PERSISTENCE OF TIME

If I live or if I die,
      Time will not stand still.
If I give that all may try,
      Time will not stand still.
If I died and had the means
To leave a will for dreams,
Souls will rejoice as time goes by
—But time will not stand still!

If you sit or if you run,
      Time will not stand still.
If you're in tuned to the drum,
      Time will not stand still.
If love matters more that life
As to fall sacrifice,
Yet tongue remains at will all dumb
—Know, time will not stand still!

If we leave upon this plane,
      Time will not stand still.
If the sun and earth remain,
      Time will not stand still.
Creation—near and far
Are all subject to a *loadstar!*
If dare we will to come again
—Know, time will not stand still!

Political Posturing

Political posturing—
Republican, Democrat, Independent
Left my heart in pain!

Pterodactyl canvassing—
Catch-as-catch-can; to the mat—emotions spent
Swept each heart for gain.

...

Less shown... the sign of *innocence:*
The quintessence of integrity;
      Lights swollen flat.

Groaned signs of abeyance,
Late fluorescence of their industry;
      White, Woman, Black.

POLITICAL SPOT-CHECK

Barrak Obama of Illinois:
  Democrat.
John McCain of Arizona:
  Republican.

Both, fresh out of the U.S. Congress
That donned the Mad Hatter's hat
And made a world of demands,
Won their party's prize:
The race of their lives—
Having been whittled down to two entries—
For the U.S. Presidency.

PRIMARY FLAVOR

Delegates and candidates
—politics, at any rate.

Democrat:
    Exhilaration!
    Quite fulfilling.
    It's about high-time!
        Long struggle—some doubt.
        Always front page on my mind.
        Fun! Good fun!
    Let's off to the *White House*;
    We've got the momentum!

Republican:
    We paved the way.
    A good eight years,
        As world economy goes!
    Sure, okay—
        A little needed repair.
    So—
    Let's make it another eight years!

RIVER CITY

The power's out, since God knows when.
Too much howling—not enough gin.
Meats... all spoiled;
Such claims the loaf.
My hands are soiled,
Nerves are toast!
And my mind is long, long bled;
Yet, on and on these winds are fed!

Came hour on, the dark claimed all.
True friend wiling—at "last call."
Sands windblown
Baptized the wave
Fifteen feet on,
Wet and grave!
At the first, when lives were tossed,
At the first were flesh-bed souls lost!

Souls cower off; lost is the "chat"
That reassured when all went black.
Winds—no rhyme,
No reason seen—
Command grave time:
Monstrous lean!
The frightened mouse's voice is heard;
The flesh, blood soul—without a word!

Fear flowers up where nothing last:
Mat fertile ground—spores are broadcasted.
Love becomes

Despondency;
And now this run
—Spoiling spree!
Full now is it the broad of day;
Winds' tidings stalk—souls in dismay!

SAIL AWAY

Sail away—
To a land of spray and surf.
Sail away—
Peter Pan, forget your worth:
 The whole world is spinning
 —Make a new beginning;
 It's all been rehearsed!
  And you don't need a degree
  Just to read history:
  All is in black and white;
  You can't make it right.
   So, sail away!
   Set soul-self free!

Sail away—
To a land where there's no night.
Sail away—
Understand, life can be bright:
 No nerves overloading
 Whiles worlds are imploding
 —It's not a sweet sight.
  And you don't need a degree
  Just to read history:
  All is in black and white;
  You can't make it right.
   So, sail away!
   Set mind's eye free!

Sail away—
To a land with running brooks.
Sail away—
From this band of Captain Hookes!
    So, why be believing
    In treasures deceiving
    Since the whole world shook!
        And you don't need a degree
        Just to read history:
        All is in black and white;
        You can't make it right.
           So, sail away!
           Live happily!

SHE ASCENDS

One in arm and one in tow
And a call to one below,
Struggles with charges to ascend
Four steps down. Twenty to attend.

At large is her elder, so
She hauls up and calls once more.

A "hail" from high, and she responds
—Is soon relieved from her alarm.
No. Her man grew no more ill.
And, no, he rests beyond the jail.
—And to hear he missed her, too!
She felt a rush she never knew....

"Yes, I'm Joe's wife. And—yes, his kids—
Little Noon! Be nice!" She smiles-- "All his."

The pride was there as she ascends.
Twelve steps more to attend.
Soon shares cares upon waiting arms—
humble embrace; she so fonds
Over this sensing face most new
"Sweet, mommy loves you, too!"

She and help just one step more—
Continues on; down two score.

And journeys long end at the door:
Tidings sweet on level floor!

SHRINKING MIDDLE CLASS

In the U.S.A.
We have a shrinking *middle class*.
It's not to say they're getting wealthy
—But poverty harassed.
  The "man of the hour"
  Championed *his* cause well,
  While mainstream U.S.A.
  Was coursed to breathe new hell!

Now all ain't okay—
Gross poverty is for the poor.
It's just that he did it all his way
—And so swung wide that door:
  The "man of the hour,"
  Persistent in all his deeds
  Could not see the "middle,"
  Refused to hear their pleas!

In our U.S.A.
The pacifying has begun.
A quarter—and the middle's happy;
Penney the poor—anon!
  The "man of the hour"
  Remembers his wealthy souls:
  Crowns wealthy U.S.A.—
  More wealth than Fort Knox holds!

Shrinking Wealth–Change

The dollar and the dime
Keeps me on my toes!
This one falls behind
With blooded nose!

Now the dime and dollar
May secure a quarter:
Can't afford the chauffeur
—Overuse of loafers!

Gold is at an all-time high
—Had floundered under 2.
Now poised at 7 and a half:
Through the roof! Who knew!

A two hundred dollar investment
In the year 2000
Two hundred and a half percent
–All profit

SHRINKING WEALTH— QUARTERLY REVIEW

Gold, at an all-time high
Had floundered under 2,
Now poised at 7 and a half:
Through the roof! Who knew!

A $200 investment
In the year 2000
Nets 200 and 1/2 percent
—All profit, my friend!

Between then and present,
Blue chips sank as lead!
Bush oil: and market's pleasant!
But soon was county bleed!

Had I just rode with gold!
Not oil nor Blue chip leads,
I'd be fondly growing old
A rich man, indeed!

Shirking Wealth—Touched Reserves

I'm never without $200 thousand:
Reserve in my breast pocket.
Fifty thousand it's become—
And I haven't even touched it!

Eight years of global see-saw;
Eight years of carousel:
"Greene-speak" with its one main flaw;
It paved our way to hell!

SOLDIER DEFINED

In heels
I hired out as "soldier;"
All they see is "girly-girl":
The very thought smacks as unfair,
And is *treasured* here as pearls!

Second
Lieuy strokes his chin, smiles:
Here I'm covered head to foot
All in green—in single file;
Yet he takes *his* second look!

In the
Field, I'm not demanding;
At our base, I do my share.
Yet, there's little understanding:
"Girly-girl" is their whole care!

I hold
My own as a soldier
For my country—under God;
Second Lieuy, as to confer,
Smiles "girly-girl" to this male squad!

SPENT

Where be the books,
That I might glean a second look!
What canopy
Would allow such atrophy?
How high the sky
That the eagle must stride
      To shut his wings
        —Unnatural thing!

No Pericles?
—Ruled heart of true Democracy?
His *golden age*:
His Athens—richly set stage!
Classical Greece:
Art, drama, philosophy
Housed by what key?
Political theory.
      Yet, here dim light's
      Lit by witless might!

A loathsome heart
May be embraced as like a god!
But things to come
Will in its own fashion;
And tarnished gold
Spends as well as burnt coal:
      Prayer to make shorn
      Is fruit likewise borne!

TECH TRAVESTY

This is a travesty!
They've buttoned up
  Basic technology:
    I'm disallowed my DVD;
    The floppy disk they took from me
      —Yet they return my gramophone!

Two gigabyte storage
Is to the bit
  As is a two-door frig
    To a single cheese wedge;
    Too soon is gone the 2/5 gig:
      Too many sit upon the throne!

THAT OLD FORD

That old Ford is still around.
Transmission froze—
Three wheels on the ground.
Yeap, it carried the load
Up town and down;
Now, it barely sits around.

Of a time this country's brand
Was known world wide
And much in demand.
Yeap, how the time does fly.
Now, all but band—
We produce by other's hands.

That of Ford done much this way.
Sparked many dreams!
It saved the U.S.A.
Yeap, it produced the cream.
Made time for play.
Now, the bite has come its way.

Fine folks say, it's dull of mind;
Making a change
Is well pass high-time!
Yeap, it's all been arranged;
Trust left behind—
Trouped in color "gee" the mind.

That old Ford is more than say;
It bears the heart
Of our own country.
Yeap, steel's Bethlehem, clocked—
Was sweep away!
Now, Ford? What'ld old Henry say?

"Whoa" the mule, he stops concerned.
Present-day news
Shows nothing is learned.
Yeap, do just as you choose—
Atlanta burned!
Me, I'd be a bit concerned.

THE GULLET

It was the gullet
   That did it
   —The gullet of a Mullet.

It struggled so,
   It nearly broke my line.

The while, it won't quit;
   My regret:
   My whole net couldn't scoop it!

Bedraggled more,
   I cut him loose this time.

THE HARVEST

I

What have you seen in Jacksonville?
 The elderly vandalized.
 Their own youth genocided.
 And red blood spilled.

What say you of this, the cause?
 Justice set aside.
 Commitment not realized.
 And human flaws.

   ...

 Predicated upon these things,
What course might be taken—
Aside from Gabriel upon the wing
And earth's foundations shaken?

 If were human flaws corrected
And nature a passing dream,
Flesh would will as would expected
—Live for his sole Supreme!

 Then the will must so respond
Beyond the dream—waking;
And the flesh can do so harm
In its under taking.

And the soul willed—spirit borne
Upon the branching tree,
Will itself the harvest sown
—Atoned, the harvest be.

Chimes and praise will ring abroad:
From heaven to Mount Zion,
Angels claiming such—*their lord,*
Leaving none behind!

II

The flesh is yet a mirror
Of His grand design
"Free will"—a *must* factor—
Must not be undermined.

Flesh without free will
Will remove all flaws
—Likewise, would make nil
The purpose of God's cause:

Redemption. Thus, upon
A Savior set apart,
Would stir no penchant,
No changing of the heart!

Faith would have no purpose
—the soul no need for prayer;
"Free will" for man—*a must,*
As all flesh needing air!

Flaws may be a burden
To all God's fleshly souls
—The flesh must toil, for certain;
Still, Christ stands in the door.

THE PACES

Everybody's pacing faster than me,
Almost like the moon is hinging on a tree—
      For them!
      I get the shade of a tiny branch;
      They get the whole limb!

You see, a one working harder of need
Must grow weary—have longing for the fancy
      Of whim!
      Luster dulled dim—as in a trance,
      With the picking's slim!

Lulling the shorn seedlings gathered, a plea
Long lost to past noon's of fading history
      Snap stems!
      As yet the while it begs romance,
      Mocks, and lights go dim!

TRUE BEARING

If you think that it is raining
and you're paining, step not aside;
the sky is broad, the road is wanting
—who doesn't know that time does fly!

If the raindrops are a bother,
consider each a universe;
take hold the helm true to the rudder,
while charting out your own true course!

Do not linger in the fallow:
it's certain planters will claim all;
take not up arms as unto battle
if not your choice as first to fall!

Do not sign on as "fair weather,"
or all you'll soon glean are turned backs;
wait not for that some unknown other—
make bearing *real*, take up the slack!

Do no pledge more than having,
else your *all* will not be enough;
seek not as center of a gathering
—if you're called, you have the *stuff!*

Make not a promise of believing:
belief is borne on faith alone;
the least of souls is worth receiving
—one justly aids from marrowbone.

As time's sun clocks it movement,
do not weary at its run;
maintain the *race* as treasured "God-sent"
—peaceable rest is sure to come.

THE BLAME'S ON ME

They blame me for no historicity:
I wore no kilt, and I wore no mail.
Here I sit in the Western jail,
Targeted for rags and "wantta be's."
When finger points—they belabor me.

They blame me for a second place home win
And question: why—after many years—
"New beginnings" is my main care:
Arrivals who are newly coming in
Make the grade; yet I just begin!

THE OTHER SIDE
OF HUMANITY

The faceless homeless on my street
Is no grand old mystery.
We got the locks and got the shorn;
Abandoned youth and aged forlorn
Have no source of drink, nor hope of meat.

Not in age old history,
In answer to prayerful appeal
God reassures Job's troubled mind!
Concerning God's own grand design.
Life is counted not all misery.

Grace, the hallmark of design
Falls away with hearts of ice.

Not in age old history;
Not as in the grand design:
About his means yet unrevealed,
In answer to prayerful appeal
God reassure Job that his woes

Did God reassure Job's troubled mind!

TO SAY

Heaven was not burped
From the belly of the whale!
T'is ludicrous to flirt
Locked away in some dank jail.

To say heart's not pained
When it's wrongly stripped from soul
Broadcasts flirtatious gains
—*Your* intent's now being fueled!

WAILING WINDS

Wailing winds, *this* Augustan noon
terrorize in waves—to soon
Is there amputated limb, shorn crown,
Assailing tears cutting to the ground!
The late blooms, at mercy to such joys,
Fret and faint—tossed as though were toys!
       And *this*, whole season 'round!

Contraband—and heart's luster lost:
Shaken, bruised brackish. This draught
Once breathed elevated lives: refreshed souls
Depleted now—broken, and, too, bound
By what course that nature stirs to hound!
Pebble, rock, granite, or towering stone,
All succumb to her winds and form!
       Prowl thus...whole season trolled!

WHY SO MUCH PAIN

I want to go where cool breezes blow;
I want to see no more misery
—Jonah, won't you send your whale for me!

I want to far fly above the sky;
I want to do something all brand new
—Archangel Michael, how about you?

I've never been the more happy when
I gave a smile to a precious child
—Now those days are all gone... ghostly miles!

Gone is the love; loyalty is snubbed;
Integrity's not a thing to be
—Archangel Michael, just pleasantries!

And what new day—can somebody say?
Oh, what of me and this tapestry
—Is it *faith* or *fate* that holds the key?

Our yesterday, all filled with dismay,
Was lost in vain—now, these sad remains
—Archangel Michael, why so much pain!

WINDY SERVICE

Know just where you are—
Though I feel your pain,
Find yourself a van or car;
I don't do no windy rains!

Cuttin' back on bus service, lady—
So, get your list in order.
Cuttin' back on bus service,
Go find an uncle or brother
—'Cause when the wind is blowin' forty,
    Don't you then dare call on me!

Cuttin' back on bus service, lady—
Not just the out-roads—all 'round!
Cuttin' back on bus service;
That means uptown and down
—If you miss your connection,
    Then, connect with next of kin!

Cuttin' back on bus service, lady—
Though I mind the "golden rule."
Cuttin' back on bus service;
Then, again, it's nothing new.
Every time my grits need gravy,
    You must know: *give* it to me!

WISHED-FOR TIME

A daring smile
Whispered a sweet "hello."
Her ample hips
Promising much more:
    A winking eye
            Insuring "on demand"
            For the *can-do* male
            With a *love-you* plan.

My loving her
Whisked in new age: *good news.*
Her mystic kiss
Disarming old blues;
    Her burning touch
            Searching heart and mind
            Beyond wishful deeds
            —Stirs up wished for time.

Our loving shared,
Peppered with "good" and "bad."
Had life-styles jelled,
While skirting the fad;
    Had tidings stayed
            Returning with her smile,
            Her heeled "can-do" male
            Would be loved the while.

YOUR SUPPLICANT

If I could *feel* your tender touch,
>I would love you even twice as much.

If I could *love* a little while,
>I would love as if it's out of style.

If I could *seed* but one sweet kiss,
>You would verily come into bliss!

If I could *gaze* into your eyes,
>Mine own heaven is soon realized.

If I could *own* your warm embrace,
>The whole world round would be mine encased.

Oh—!
Just one turned smile...
>—I languish here the while.

GIRL FROM VIEW

Matenopoulos
And yet Man's betroth!
Not more hour this
But this moment—*bliss!*

Man's soul loosed on froth!
—*Swee*t Matenopoulos!

ONE MORE DAY AND
WHERE SHE BE?

No girl I got
I got no friend.
   Only got the world
   I'm not living in.

One Black pearl
And lost to sin!
   Pushed wheel borrow's
   My state of motion.

With no way I got
I got no care
   Only get to say
   I'm barely here.

Talk one more fray.
And this I fear:
   Will come the day
   "I just don't care!"

So–

Don't *how* tell me.
I got to live!
   I've been given
   Out before.

Can't now well say
I'm up to give
   Got no more
   Letting go!

Oh!--

One Black pearl
One pip away.
   Only had a girl
   To make my day!

"Your girl I am!"
She'd say–"*Your* friend.
   All the world we got
   For living in!

"Say, Don't *how* tell!
We got to live!
   We've been given
   Out before!"

Can then 'loud say
Life's more to give.
   With so much more!
   Baby, let's go!

PEOPLE OF COLOR

--Song--

People of Color--
Colored, Negro, Black man. Yeah.
When will you wake up,
and fill you place in destiny.

We are Balalian.
You can wake up, should you choose.
Together as one,
with color and pride, we just can't lose.
We Are Balalian.
Come... fill your own destiny.

SPRINGTIME PARADISE

I walk short Spring in verdant paths
where roses pressed a dew-dropped bath--
saluted day with rave reviews.

The earth stood still; my cares took flight–
as soul strung filled with pure delight!
All life infused!

TO BE NEGRO

To be Negro...
Why see myself
As hodgepodge
of persons else?

There's yet wealth
—*Keys musical*--
To see myself
As sole Negro!

PEOPLE ARE MOVING

--Song--

People are moving--and going places...
By cars and by planes and trucks;
On buses and trains--on foot.
Oh--
But the disgrace is
Nobody cares.
Nobody bares
The pain of his brother
The burdens he suffer
No...!
--Nobody cares....

PROSE

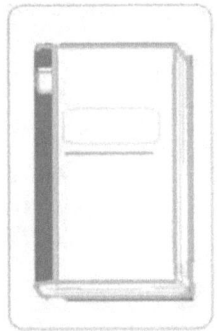

THE CHARTREUSE WALL

by
Mitchell Alexander Jackson

Part I

Exclusion breeds community. This was a different type culture, a different type seasoning, a different rumored life-style: a submergence well advanced of any eminent ambrosia. More at being a sharpen embolus in an emollient society that neither command nor reprimand, the individual was-- here--garnished wholly; thus is embraced the intellectual and the non-intellectual, the political and the non-political. And not discounted among these few were the wealthy and its counter-part--as if for some arcane purpose.

No longer facing a flagellant society having flagrant intent, the seasoned and novice had yet to wean themselves of centuries of fear. Could a son of ancient Gomorrah image himself beyond the mirror in to a more palatable, sympathetic reality--experiencing no longer the paradigm of fish bowl *and* fish pond? As society stumbled amid hapless *and* contrived confusion, the exclusion of this arena of society gleaned a glimmer, and darkness fell away, leaving merely shadows of an undefined constellation and a consternation to be fielded by these selfsame denizens of their own questioned self-prejudices.

...

A primer such as this propelled the young man upon his way through a boreen spiked by wicked, il-matched baleen-like strips resembling a fence. Unrestrained board-foot too often threatened his person, as rye grass tendril-like fretted about his ankle boots.

As the young man made his way on foot, he thought that maybe he should have accepted the Madame's gracious offer. She had hired him expressly as a mobile companion. "She hired me to fetch and carry," he grumbled to himself. "There's nothing wrong with driving the car when she is not in it."

Another step, another thought: If he's not driving the woman about, she still has him picking up this parcel or dropping off some other, he had once remarked to Shannon. But his rejecting the use of the car meant more than a simple "thank you, no." The woman's aloneness *or* sweet-heart remembrances pivoted her social intent. Such could influence her "gifting." The woman's reserve, cultural differences, class ranking must not be placed in jeopardy. Should she, in one insane instance, appeared to have compromised her position of grand respectability, could he survive?

This was, in deed, a thorn for the young man. As he was not certain if he could but succumb to the invitation. For the matron's wealth was as a magnet to persons in his economic condition. He would become of a certainty--if his resolve should fail completely, or confusion should usurp his propensity for independence--a kept retainer; if his were the ability to *perform*.

When she first touched him "meaningfully," he quickly pulled away. Not fearing the touch, but his very identity. It was almost as though she had sensed that he had known no field, experienced no stream; understood he nothing of the plowing nor the sowing. And confused pandemonium heaped upon him as his fears escalated. Disquietude pummelled his feelings of insecurity and left him, often times blanched, drained--except for the unrelenting, ambiguous fear.

"Shannon, Regina, now Mrs. Otum--" he shook his head, as he kicked a pebble from beneath his feet. Stopping, he looked into the distance. Yet another ribbon of tattered fences: of board; of wire--hooked a disenchanting presence across the red-green landscape. Beyond he could almost see his destination--with the elevation becoming more apparent. He trailed onward, with red dust whipping about his trousers, and fears confounding his kinship of soul's self.

...

Peter Dugan righted himself as though discovering a sudden thought lodged between his temples. The unsure front legs of the wooden chair struck the checkered green and white tile floor in sharp retort. But he seemed not to notice the loud squeaks and unsteady response. In stead, he reached for the receiver. The smile stretched the width of his face, as the eyes popped wide with awareness. Just as suddenly, he returned the receiver and pushed the phone out of reach. *No. He must wait.* Pearlee was just beyond the door. What if she should walk in or should overhear? She's forever telling him how he needs to put his spine to work and act like a man. "Employ that sacroiliac," he muttered absently.

He busied himself with an emerald, pocket size book-- flipped a page; returned; then snapped the book shut. He took one last look at the sparse pages and then consigned the minor dissatisfaction to a more pleasing recourse.

"Hep, hep! Pepey! Yi--two points!"

"Is your end ready for later? Ramey's sending over the Piraruco."

The woman Pearlee caught his at his reveling. She did not bother to enter into the office the two of them shared together.

"Eh– Sure. Yeah, got everything right here," the man said.

"I hope to have an inductee tonight. And, of course, you will shepard the young man?"

It was a statement--not a request.

"Eh--"

"Initiator, Peter! And you really must do more with your demeanor. I ply you with books I feel you can manage. That is the key word, Peter. *Manage*. The more one explores the written word, the better one is apt to organize one's own thoughts. Ergo, *manage!*

"Oh, get off it! I'm not impressed."

"I suppose it takes a modicum of intellect to germinate intelligence. Oh--" The woman tossed over her shoulder as she walked off, "You may return *Pepey*," then disappeared from view.

Peter supposed that the woman had witnessed his deed. And he further supposed how she could improve on her own disposition. "If she wants it, let her fetch it. Bow-*wow*," he said emphatically.

Still were there things to be readied, tasks to get gone, and the gathering of like souls were but a short while away. Peter reversed his thinking on reserving the "fetch" task for the woman; he *employed* his sacroiliac."

...

The young man, engrossed in thought, soon found the hour upon him. For suddenly, there stood the wall--stalwart and rectangular, as grass scurried along its southern border. Thought flooded anew. The wall stood twenty-two feet in length and was capped at approximately nine feet. It was strapped at intervals of six feet approximations with shallow buttresses; and were these housed double inset panels between each—such were the notable architectural features. The entire wall was covered with Portland plaster. But what was most striking about the wall was its patina and incised pattern. The color had varying episodes of yellow-greens; and the pattern flaunted an abstract floral design. The coloring, though kindred to nature, appeared alien on the wall. *And the wall, in turn, appeared alien to its natural surroundings.*

The abrupt squaring of recesses and their compliments, the buttresses, shackled the very essence of what is natural and instigated a strange, hallow placidness. The wall celled in its occupant--the dwelling. This wall promulgated a compensatory persona that was merely a facade, as the tops of the windows squinted over its rim.

"Yeah," the young soul murmured to himself. "There is something that does not love a wall." He attempted to shake off the affects of its strangeness upon his presence. "What can it mean...?" He coasted into reality: "Well, I'm here," he said.

It was dusk–8:20 pm. The young man gave each boot the once over: he dusted away the tara cotta film until the black shown lack-luster at the heel and toe; he applied saliva from lip to handkerchief—treatment for scuff marks unsightly, abusive.

"It'll have to do," he said, when realizing that a damp tap at the trousers would worsen their present state. "Not even the excuse of bachelorhood would make soiled trousers acceptable."

Hesitantly, he knocked upon the door. He rang the bell.

Presently, the door opened on a claret visage. His short-cropped hair was echoed by the tailored, red beard. "Hi. I'm Peter Dugan. You, I recall. You must be Shannon's friend." A full-tooth smile winked on... profusely.

"Corey Wonders--"

"Peter--! To you." Again that effervescent smile. "Come in. Come in!"

As the young man was allowed to squeeze pass his host, the smile beamed its delight. *The waiting was over.* A delicate touch urged the visitor onward.

...

That she was female alpha went without question. Her thirty-nine years invested her with a physical grace that many felt compelled to respect and an intellect that few could ignore. She never failed an opportunity to advance the females within her group. Always she responded to each and the other's needs. From the implied to the expressed, she groomed her charges in the intricacies of *intent.* Highly charged, she was yet reserved; conservative yet liberal: an enigma. Political in cause but submissive (hierarchically) in course, too often she would bite her lip--hold her tongue--and encourage the male, Peter, to dominance; though she considered him inadequate. Though bi-polar in most things, in this one thing was she not: intimacy. It was in this one area her feelings spiralled strongest; in this one area her intellect was least adequate.

In this female of females, woman of women, intimacy registered zero in response to male gender. Thus, she may "come off" as "bitch","dike","butch." But the essence of her thoughts, being, had been captured by the mysteries which are female. Pearlee made no fanfare, gave no parade, but with sole devoutness–in love, as Dido? And not just a Sappho.

She stood up and strolled over to the punch bowl, meats, cheeses, nuts, chips, finger sandwiches, dips, sauces, salad-stuffs, and all manner of trimmings. Raising a short-stem wine glass from the smorgasbord linen-draped table that fronted the room, she then lightly struck its rim with a salad fork. Stillness hushed all. Then spoke Pearlee.

"Welcome all, to our little excursion of who we are. Welcome to *Maffick*. And now--" The woman drew the last word out into an anticipatory pause. At this moment, Peter, on cue, stepped forward. "And now," she resumed, "varsity trans-genders give you--tonight's affair of Look-See. I give you your host, Peter Dugan."

Applauds. *Dugan*. More applauds. And still the shouts: *Dugan! Dugan!*

Finally, the woman stepped forward. There was a note of displeasure on her face. She, this second time, sounded a singular maestro note upon the wine glass; Peter Dugan lamentably acknowledged his cue to begin the festivities--the captive audience expressed a sign of relief and anticipation.

"Peter! And what was that little bit of trivia? Even I felt Chaucerian--a hostage whose person was being demeaned. If you intend to play the captor, please place greater value on my worth."

"Meaning--?" Peter frowned. The brainy type made him to feel inappropriate, somehow.

"Bromide, Peter, having your group of "soldiers" to degrade themselves that way. Make it something of relevance next time. *Please,* don't waste everybody's time."

Peter Dugan watched as the woman fanned her way amongst the celebrants.

"No amount of verve makes that woman to glitter. Perfection just isn't in her," he fumed His eyes fell upon the young woman at the far side of the gathering. If he hadn't been a consummate consanguinity--men only, she would have been the ideal mate. She was physically unsurpassed in a feminine way. A voluptuous dancer and songstress. He was sometimes haunted by the girl's affect on him--female to male, in search of that special someone.

Sometimes he had regrets that he had not made the effort. He often experienced the guilt of seeing--knowing--he obediently placed her in the hands of *that* woman. he felt marked... responsible for her present fortune. For that woman not only took full advantage of this precious, compliant individual, but she tossed her off, as one would out-of-vogue apparel--and for a woman ten years the girl's senior! And now the disheartened girl has been passed on to that bitch, Toolah. Toolah--who has presently been reduced the girl to suppliant groanings.

He knew Toolah to be volatile. He suspected her to be somewhat unstable--perhaps, suicidal. He was aware of the rumors. The woman was connected to criminal elements! "My duty. I should--" he mutter to himself. But, perhaps, a safer route, he waged to himself, would be to issue a written complaint and possibly have that woman expelled from the group. "The community would be better off without her." Still, there must be the initial confrontation. No one is turned out without an opportunity to address the party bringing forth the complaint. He knew he did not have the constitution for such a confrontation, nor its likely ramifications. He set himself to witness the turning of the minutes upon hour.

As the night wore on, Shannon canvassed the room from a small enclave that allowed access to a hall transversing the back of the building. The dwelling was one of these butchered events that had suffered additions and extensions and a general dishearten ignorance of primeval esthetics. Still, this particular hall had been given inordinate philanthropies. No tidth nor tiddle was spared. The broad emerald band of paisley trailing two feet from the ceiling of inlaid panelling; with panelling boxing planarly pictures exotica; such etching along the upper two feet, with greater design and measure played out upon the vastness of the spacious wall area.

Thus, from this vantage point, Shannon commanded an extensive view of the room and its occupants. The regulars were there: Peter could be heard crowing above the din; Pearlee could be seen brooding over her "chicks." Also, could Toolah be seen aping her intentions from one small cluster to the next; likewise, Regina, as usual, could be seen hugging the bar and something resembling a screw-driver; then there were Morgen and Millie, Catherine, Limpkin, Tranz, Orpheus, and numerous others weaving throughout the faceless--the nameless.

But Shannon had just one person ravishing his thoughts. His face blazed whit-hot and his name ever pulsated, heat immersed--and unrelenting--stoked Shannon's soul to the point of--

"Do--" Shannon breathed in a quiet voice, "'Less you burn!"

Shannon's breath faltered, as young Corey came into view. Just as sudden, an inner mobility refused Shannon the opportunity to welcome Corey--to claim him, to cling to him with whole meaning and expression of one whose love--vulcanized--knows no limits. If only Shannon could now go to him, to touch him--all so often opportunities had gone untouched--from the first, when Shannon felt the warmth of Corey's gaze during that first Psychology 101. To feel Corey's arms... to experience his lips... to taste his freshness.... Such thoughts, and their impossibility only amplified the aching, clouded identity of self, and devastated resolve. And the only thought to register through the tears, the pain, as Shannon turned a tearful face to the inner recesses of a shadowed, beige existence--devastated him now:

"Least you shall burn..."

It was *impoda grada*, with outward evidence of a solitary tear engulfed in shadows.

In the main gathering, Corey was all attentive. The festivity, Corey thought, had a strained air about it. And though his host trouped himself before gracious recipients, he found it difficult to warm up to this special gatherers. One reason for this insane feeling was the ever-pressing "passes" received from his host; a second was the prying thought that Shannon was deliberately avoiding him. These reasons alone made Corey unable to feel "freely uninhibited" towards those he met. Pearlee he spotted from a distance. And he stole a moment during an inclusive "chat" to spot-check about the room.

"Myrtle...."

She smiled. Encouragement shown in her eyes. All the while, she could feel Toolah's eyes burning into the nape of her neck. She had imbibed a little too recklessly, and now she was full-throttled. A giggle pirouetted across her lips and a hand attempted to retrieve an at large hiccup.

It encored a giggle, which urged on an "excuse do" wave of the fingers. The neophyte type response by the young Corey was acknowledgment enough. That timid, insecure vulnerability of the young man warmed her immeasurably. The girl's smile broaden.

"My--!" Her thoughts shimmered, as the colored lights reflected upon the surface of the near-by pond. But she deciphered them clearly. There--Pearlee intercepting her lover.... Young Corey toying with the idea that she could be his tonight and looking luscious... and she feeling insane! Wow! And, of course, Toolah! Goodman Toolah! While she was still desirable, she desired true manliness; then, especially. Let Toolah prat and fume. In the beginning, she desired Peter--gentle, kind, warm Peter. But, once again she settled. Settled... settled.... That word bombarded her tentative, liquid-like thoughts, clouding the lights... lights.

"Oh--!" It felt as though her brain had managed a three-sixty. She tried not to register the tics of each degree, for she intended to maintain a clear head, enough to have her own intent fulfilled. "If not the naive Corey--"

She tried but could not to spot him on the floor.... She panned the room for her second choice. The youthful twenty-three year old--wholesome--a kind of purity she had not experienced since.... Maybe, being with Toolah was her problem. The thought was barely out before... fallacy. She had been messed up before the Toolah era. Still, she could not understand why she needed someone in her life–any someone. And her *self* was ever being demolished. "But, that crazed witch--!"

Tonight she would have her own way. "I claim tonight! Tonight--" she struggled with hesitant thoughts.

"Tonight...." The thought kept looping to its beginning, it seemed. *Tonight.... Tonight....*

"Tonight...."

Toolah attempted to signal to Myrtle from across the room and saw the other woman return gaze make a deliberate detour. Toolah directed her line of sight at the object of intrusion.

Corey felt the imposing glare. He turned. The young man could hardly expect anything amiss, the woman Toolah impressed an icon of contempt upon his senses.

"Watch your step." Her words were nowise audible, yet they were un-mistakenly clear. The "Or else" went un-mouthed, but not unrealized for the young man. As the baffled Corey tried to make sense of the sudden hostility, the exchange did not go unnoticed. Pearlee wasted no time intervening.

"Girl-friend, please. Ladies are poised. We girls must maintain the feminine mystique."

"We girls--"

The woman Pearlee gently stroke the other's forearm. "Now, Toolah. Young Corey had been with us less than a week. He hasn't had time to get to know us--to appreciate our way, our style in living. Let's afford him more time, okay?"

"Time--!" Toolah could no longer contain herself. "Myrtle is off limits. Hear me? She's mine!"

"You know the rules, here." Pearlee struggled to medigate the edge to her voice. "We do not restrict the individual--Jack or Jill. Tonight, the rule is *recourse,* Toolah. And young Corey is okay. In fact, I intend to invite him to my political endeavors."

"I don't care about the who, what, or why-- Myrtle... *is* mine."

Pearlee deliberately stepped into the other woman's personal space. "The rules, Toolah."

Toolah felt the graveness of the matter, inadvertently back-stepped.

"How you conduct yourself in private is your affair; but here at Chartreuse, it's mine. I see that you're again into leather," said the older woman, flatly. "Toolah, if I should suspect that you're in any way connected with 'hot' goods, you're out of her. And if I should hear that you are by any means responsible for burglaries, your behind's bought a county cell, lady!"

"You don't have the right to make me out a thief!" Toolah was piqued with irritable anger. And she brandished it with unrivaled iridescence.

"Make?" Pearlee was not unfamiliar with the erratic tantrums. She stood her ground. I do not *make* you, Toolah. I am *aware* of you. And I shall continue to be so."

The younger woman broke away without an utterance. A priming thought yet upon the forge, she carried not with her that smallest kernel of fear--only the anger, storing up, reworking... reserved. And a smarmy smile arrested the countenance of this woman's face.

...

She had known Corey three days, and already she could hardly wait for his return visit. He was the sole thought that reduced her mental acuity to absent-mindedness. "Uh-- What was that?"

"Baby, you're just not with me today-- I know...." Pearlee reached over and caressed the other woman momentarily--hair... face. "Pearlee's going to fix her sugar some coffee."

A microwave oven made quick work of the chore. Pearlee shortly returned with a service and tray. The interval had been too short; for Regina's thoughts of the young man wad once again disrupted.

"There. Just as yuou like it. *Coffee Ole*. Not that *Mokca* crap. And, of course, with a shot of Bourbon. Now, tell me what's troubling my dear-heart." Pearlee was too happy to gift the warmest of smiles as she planted the tray on the bed.

The girl hesitated: hands fixed about her cup and words fixed in her throat.... "You met him. Now--now, don't get angry with me. But, gosh-- I mean, he's so--so...."

"Intriguing?"

Pearleel's expression is deadpan.

"Yeah. I--I guess so. He makes me forget myself. Know what I mean? I think if him constantly. Can't sleep, but he's in my imaginings... holding me real, real close. And the fire--!"

"Regina! Hush! Nonsense. He isn't--" The older woman halted, next pleaded. "You can't be serious! I-- We... we've always been enough for each other."

"Maybe. But it ain't like we ever went our private way. Off together like. You do your thing and I do mine."

"We do have occasion to entertain desperately. But this is different. *This is dangerous.* You mustn't--can't see him. I forbid it!"

"But we've already made plans to--"

"You will not! Hear me! Just *mustn't...!*" This last plea was delivered through a flood of tears.

The paining, tearful Regina slowly sank back into the crimson silks of the pillows, as Pearlee's watery coos and coddling attempted to drown to overflowing the unquenchable.

Part II

Two days earlier they had talked. Agreed, perhaps? Now was Corey at a loss as to why he had not heard from Regina. She had broached the subject of being "regulars." Going steady, maybe? When he first came into contact with this crowd, he had hoped that they would alley his fears and flood the confusion. *Is he...? Or isn't he?* He needed an answer. But things had gone all the more wrong. Regina and he–he knew–could build a wonderful life together. She was in a position to understand his perplexity and he was aware enough to appreciate complex needs. Still, love rules the house. He could become Man personified and she Woman. Their own regeneration of the new Adam and his Eve were but sparks away. But she had refused to see him. Or to say *why.*

"Why...?"

Why in this confusion was he evolving towards the inexplicable? On the one side was *love.* On the other, *Shannon.* Should the inexplicable were to meet dead center: *love* and *Shannon.* "Man personified? I'm just a blubbering baby!" Corey said, choking back a tear. And yet the attraction for Shannon was there. His Shannon question remained always: *male, female*?

Corey needed clear answers–but was issued none. It was apparent to most of the community that Corey had never experienced love. And they fanned about as flies. And from the first, Shannon had attached himself to Corey. From the beginning was Shannon friendly, but evasive. "Just say, No." Shannon had once advised Corey. So why was he, Corey, here? And why was it that his feelings seem to have grown... escalated... towards his "special" friend.

Diversion? Or inevitable? These two questions raced about Corey's thoughts--until being overshadowed by another.

"Why doesn't Regina return my call?"

Presently, Corey surveyed the room for any hint of her. It was not that he didn't know what he wanted. He wanted no part of peter. There was no confusion there. For him, the answer had always been *no*. And he knew that his inexperience desired his first taste of fruit to be female proper. No confusion there, as well. But-- But why were human feelings so entangling? Now, there is Shannon and confusion.... The thought made Corey feel as though he were betwixt and between--the male soul struggling to establish self. Thus the cloud of confused perplexity continued to orchestrate an aura of fear and uncertainty.

Still, Corey looked the room over. He noted Toolah, no Shannon, no Myrtle... and no Regina. The merry-makers were now sparse. This usually meant that the individual desires were being paired off--coupled--in the various "rooms of destiny." Perhaps, that was why God and self blared confusingly dull and drone. Corey sighed, made his way to the nearest exit. From this gala of communal bliss, Corey homeward departed.

He pulled the Lincoln into the dirt and gravel lot. In his state dejection, Corey had neglected to give the Lincoln's interior the once-over, especially the rare seat. With the luxuriant Continental parked beneath the oak, the dishearten Corey chastised himself for having taken the car. He felt that he had failed himself. He felt guilt-ridden, somehow.

Even now did Corey not give the car a backwards glance, as from her vantage point of the plush rare seat of the Lincoln, Myrtle could see the silhouette intercept the engrossed, departing Corey.

"Oh! It's you."

"Been thinking, Corey."

"Yeah." Corey sensed what was coming. "Me, too," he added. Ever since meeting the charming Shannon, Corey had tried to circumvent it; yet were his secret yernings... of consummation. The both steered into the shadow.

Behind her private window Myrtle set puzzled, then suddenly caught sight of a mild disturbance. She watched as this couple strolled through, dissecting the grounds to enter the dwelling. She had caught snatches of banter as they passed. Perhaps a "she." And a definite "waiting." But little more.

"Eh--" The silhouette had emerged.

The two paused, looked in the direction of the dwelling.

"I--I wanted to..." the silhouette continued. "To show you how I feel. To let you know--" His hand felt out the shoulder of Corey's left arm; and Corey felt a sudden bolt of excitement. An explosion tracked nerves and fibers of his body.

"Shannon, I--"

The pause became interminable.

Shannon's heart ached in the glaring silence. Yet his heart would not allow him the luxury of turning away. And so, he stumbled to mouth the dictates of his heart. But he came short of reciting that all-evoking sentiment. No *I love you*. Instead, he managed only, "I'm *your* friend. And I'll be here for you."

It's said that *Silence is golden*. But for Shannon, it was a glaring condescension, toppling dreams from heights of truest feelings, to languish as something less than perfectly belonging. To add greater weight to purpose his postulation, albeit, it would insure greater pain in his torment, he squeezed Corey's arm and pressed his lips most tenderly against the mute face. Next did Shannon turn and was gone.

Myrtle had used the advantage of the two men's involved discourse to abandon the rare seat and car. From fractured shadows she witnessed Shannon's departure. She decided then to allow Corey time to settle into his apartment before revealing herself. Barely could she maintain her patience as Corey turned the lock, next the knob--and entered beyond the door.

The quiet stillness reached from out the semidarkness and grasp the unsuspecting Corey.

"Ah! I was hoping that battle-royale would end earl."

The voice was enough to stir the startled Corey in a moment of raptured elation! "Regina!" he whispered.

In the overcast partial darkness, the girl brushed a kiss against his check. "Just a hint of what's to come."

He could almost make out her smile. The promise was so inviting, the unlocked door was neglected as the found couple made their way up the stairs to his bedroom.

Through the upstairs window a small blue light defused the darken room with flashes of brilliance. The young woman disrobed. Clad only in bikini briefs, she began undoing the young man of his clothing--steering him onto the unpretentious bed while doing so. Each step was rewarded with a gyrating promise from her body against his own. Man felled upon the bed. Each button undone was graced with a turn of womanly gyrations. Cast of belt and undone fly intensified gyrations! Trousers he aided in kicking free. How well--fitting--her mouth found his. Lips, tongues locked in embrace! How sweetly did her breasts sought out the hardness of his chest! Her flesh burn into his own! And no wall between them but the sheerest of briefs...!

...

In the briefest of seconds, Myrtle's patience had abandoned her. With great hesitancy she charted a round-about route through the shadows. Having reached the front door, she offered up a small prayer. *The door was ajar!* With spark now kindled ablaze, the driven woman bounded up the few steps and through the open door way!

The anticipating Myrtle made her way up the stairs. With marine-like stealth she discovered Corey's room door without alarming the house. A quiet turn of the knob proved this door to be unlocked. Myrtle entered. The pleasures of the woman's design grew ice cold! Was there the immediate awareness of impassioned breathing... perfume... commingling aroma Aphrodite. Light bantering from without revealed the couple's heavily orchestrated movements of rapture.

Suddenly was there sobbing--that of Myrtle and the passionate Regina--Eve stoking the fires within her Adam! Strength was drained from Myrtle of a sudden! Yet legs, brain, tears declared their independence as the devastated Myrtle mustered what strength she could, turned, and raced from the apartment house. Wooden legs gave little support as the confused, tearful woman poured out her heart into the stillness and the night.

A sudden pain of a different type struck the woman fully in the face! A second blow to the stomach sank the woman to her knees. A hand reached down and ripped at a mass of hair, heaved the head backwards. A resounding slap cracked across her face.

"Slut!" the enraged voice cried out.

The young woman had been rendered senseless from the pain. Was she barely conscious. Only a type of babble and blood trickled from her lips. A witness to the horror of the assault could have testified to unbridled hatred, lust and fear. That witness could have attested to the savagery, pain and powerlessness incurred. But there was none on the grounds. Instead, was there Toolah with the near lifeless body in tow. She dragged Myrtle to her El Camero and tossed the body rag-doll style into the car.

Still, the atrocity did not go unwitnessed. Regina, at the upstairs window, hugged herself tightly as the assault came to an end. The savagery had displaced the warmth, security of the shared enlivened escapade. Presently, she felt her body shiver involuntarily as she watch Toolah drive off with her victim. A grave look over her shoulder witnessed the prostrated Corey beneath the covers, caught up in sleep. Her Orpheus... Morpheus slain--dead to the world. Suddenly were her fears compounded. And the tremors would not go away.

···

Toolah was not satisfied with her act of reprisal. She "encouraged" Myrtle to tell all. And she felt betrayed. How dear she look at another! And that Shannon bitch! "How could she share the same love interest with that--" For her, it was unthinkable. She knew what she must do! She threw herself upon the hapless woman for the last time.

···

Shannon awoke to feel a hand cut across his face. Then all went black.

...

Corey could not believe the events of the preceding night. Yet, here he was being questioned. He looked up in to the solemn face that had earlier insisted he be escorted *down town*.

"Poor Myrtle... dead?" He fingers folded about themselves. "But, Shannon? No, sir--" he said emphatically. "I can't believe he can do that kind of thing."

The lead officer's disinterested expression were suddenly piqued. "Look, Mr--eh, Wonders. We have everything we need." He placed the pen squarely upon his desk, sighed heavily. "Just loose ends. Don't need your personal beliefs--just a statement. Case close."

"But, I don't understand. You can't have anything against Shannon. He--"

The officer snorted, then frowned. "We've got evidence, motive, and a body. And it all points to your friend. Now, Mr. Wonders, if you don't mine...."

Corey shifted in the plastic seat. He wanted to rise, to race for the exit. But the metallic chair held, grounded him; or was it the fear of appearing afraid? Strangely enough, a thought of Peter flickered pass. "I really can't see how, in less than twenty-four hours, the police can be sure of who did it."

The office harnessed a laugh. Then smiled, Instead. "Look. We have pubic hair samples, semen. Son, we even got blood and tissue samples. *And* we got Laceman, there, at the scene. The only thing we're not sure about is whether or not he--she? Eh, had an accomplice."

This last statement was meant to intimidate. But Corey tried to ignore it.

"Fingerprint?"

"Don't need'em. We can place him at the scene of the crime."

"But motive--"

"Look. It's good that a guy like him has a friend-- Pal-- Buddy. You know what I mean. But if the Lieutenant say we got'em? We got'em!" The seated officer reared back in the ancient chair. "Motive? See these--sergeant stripes. I've been around. Listen up. We've seen all kinds. A man kills his baby because the kid get more of the wife's time than he's allotted. A man shoots another man for taking a bite out of his burger. A woman slices off her husband's preck because-- Well, you get the picture."

"Sir, Corey reiterated, "What about Shannon?"

"Yeah, well, for us, motives don't change. Our job is to fit the right sleaze to the right motive."

As the sergeant forced a leash about his temper, the controlled measure of that last statement made it evident to Corey that the officer was not comfortable with the thought of being challenged. Corey lean back in his seat, as if to make the golf between them greater.

"Strange people--" the officer–composed–continued. "Do strange things. For strange reasons. And the way we got it figured, your strange, eh–unique friend was having a tussle with himself. Psychological like. Like Jacob in the wilderness--"

"What's the Bible has to do with anything?"

The officer appeared flustered. "Scheeze! People demand a motive. Then don't understand it when they hear it." He sucked in some air, blew it out. "No. Not the Bible, as such. And I was told you're one of the smart ones. Son, its like this. A kind of self examination. Anyway, you friend goes to the young lady for help. It's a *man thing*. You see? He *is*. But he *ain't*. And this is--"

"Sergeant Coffee!" the voice boomed form nowhere.

There was no mistaking the voice of authority. Corey had half risen and the desk sergeant had snapped to full attention.

"Who's in charge here...?" the newly arrived officer glowered at the two uniformed officers with reserved disdain, then retreated to an inner office. Corey chose that moment to hasten on his way, risking only a backward glance.

Too close to home had been the sergeant's surmise. Corey knew that his name could have been substituted for that of Shannon's and the supposition would have rung true. But he was no longer caught up in the web. He felt free! Where Shannon had failed, he himself had succeeded.

...

Regina! Life. Breath. Soul. Pause of his end's beginning. Passion of his being.

The thankful thoughts of gratitude tracked about in his mind. But what of deliverance? The inquiry continued to resurface, as shadows of night played about the walls of his room, opening voids of doubt. The thought nagged suspiciously about the eaves of his mind to rob him of real peace. The grounds for such suspicions came from Regina's own lips; and it had only been three days since the horrific incident. Yet did she not say she vowed herself to Pearlee? Prostrated upon his bed, could he recall clearly:

"But I can't give up Pearlee. What, with Myrtle's death. Pearlee and Myrtle used to have a thing going. She is even now crushed."

He could also recall his own response:

"I--I know. But I don't see how that affect us--what *we* have together. A wonder life, Regina! Think of it, we can--"

He recall how too suddenly she had cut him off--as if to take a dream and forever lock it out:

"Don't! Can't you understand?"

He recalled the tenderness of the hour, as she leaned into him, brushed her lips against. The sound of her voice, her body fragrance came rushing on, pooling about his senses, as he remembered, even then, their pledges of love:

"...Love you", she had insisted. "And I want you to feel whole... complete."

He recalled how his own body responded, shifting to return a like measure of pleasure. How both bodies lapped at each other--and he recalled the warmth, oneness, as he toyed kissed upon her wet flesh.

The presence of that hour chilled over as Corey recalled the damning evidence. It was during a relaxed moment, each wrapped in the warmth of the other. Then those words:

"Well--"

His Eve paused, propped on her elbow as she gazed into his eyes. The pause grew questionably lengthy. Corey could sense something wrong. Re recalled her giving him the most tender spark of a kiss. Then:

"That's what I need, too. You can only be *this* part of me. I need Pearlee."

"No, Regina," Corey said aloud, as recall his rebutal. "You don't need Pearlee. Not in that way. Don't--don't wall me out...!"

But Regina had had a rebuttal of her own:

"My Corey... I'm different. Can't you see that--? That if it's not Pearlee, it'll be somebody else? Look. If you want me in your life, call me. But, I'm not going to short-change myself. Not just so you can feel like a man. *As is,* Corey. Or nothing!"

After that, it was as if Regina was a different person entirely. What did she mean when she said *Even the grander love must endure?* And everything beyond that point had grown alien to him. He recalled she rising from bed, stepping into her skirt, and suggesting that he give her proposition some thought. And how alien it sounded, after witnessing this different woman arrange her blouse, step into her shoes, to hear her say "I do love you."

The next instance she was gone.

Presently lay Corey in stillness, darkness abounding. For one short moment he thought he heard the beating of his tortured heart; but it was the raucous sobs curdling from out his throat.

...

Peter Dugan set at his desk and propped his feet on the sill. He did not bother to look out the window. He smiled at the thought, as he reached for a pencil. He scripted the capital "P." He followed this with an "e." With leisurely pace he scripted out the name. "Pearlee, you are altering. First, the loss one venerate friend," he paused, savoring the thought, "--and is losing hold of your present flame!"

He absently tapped the pencil's tip against the page of a bounded legal pad. "Showing signs of weakness. Ever on her guard. I could get nothing passed that woman. But--" He flipped the pencil with an air of expertise. The pencil was maneuvered into a slow cadence, its eraser drumming against the same page. "Her defenses are only as good as her constitution is strong."

Resented her, he did. He could always expect to be the target of one of her putdowns. And she always found and audience for her little twists of the blade. The thought fueled his enmity toward the woman. How can a follow maintain respect before the troop? "Well, now," decided Peter, "It's my turn. You insisted that I take charge...."

He liberated his feet, set them squarely on the floor.

"Employ by sacroiliac?" He raised to his full seated position, squared his shoulders. "When I am done--" Peter smiled to himself. "She will be destroyed!" And then, as if recalling a private joke he recited: "'I'll strike while the iron is hot!'"

Thus, in short order, Peter Dugan convoked a secret meeting and persuaded the board that Miss Pearlee Moss was on longer effective to administer the office of sitting president. The ousted Pearlee was replaced by Peter Dugan, whose greatest delight was in administering this point of fact to the deposed Pearlee. The office of President carried with it an automatic co-chairman position--the second great delight for the newly installed Peter. This meant that Peter could choose the interim counterpart *and* influence the selection of the permanent co-chairman. Where once hours passed in the office space had been a headache for Peter, to say the least, presently hours sailed on in near quiet bliss. The greater of Peter's joy?

"I--I don't understand--?" Pearlee had fought back tears as she cleared out her meager office possessions.

"Neither does anyone understand that Versace, Cunannan thing a few years back." Peter lustered up fain sympathy: *But dead is dead*, he thought. His smarmy disposition tickled his sense of finality. He had watched ceremoniously as the distraught woman make her retreat.

"And she can believe, with that crazy Toolah grieving her own loss, mother hen Pearlee is just so much *history!* Smile he did; and the smile triumphantly had broadened.

Peter presently rocked by in his chair, hand cupped behind his head, ignoring the immediacy of the hour evidenced by open files and papers upon his desk. "Count all bliss the absence of the office presence of one Pearlee Moss."

He smiled, just a little. Then all joy touched his soul.

"Just... like... a wo-*man*... But she crum-*bles*...." To himself quietly he sang, of a familiar tune, "Like... a little gir-*erl!*"

...

The gathering was abruptly cut short because Toolah, dazed and contrary, was too much herself. As the last of the gatherers departed, Peter Dugan maneuvered Toolah into office.

"Sit down. Please, Toolah," Peter gestured from his chair.

"Look, I'm not up to no crap." Toolah said defensively. And she wore the earmarks of loneliness and bereavement.

"Sorry about your loss."

"What's it to you?"

"Pearlee's hurting, too, Toolah."

"Not half as much... as when I'm through."

Peter ignored the guardedness in the woman's voice. "Pearlee's no longer mistress of the *Chartreuse.*"

"Get to the point."

"Well, Toolah. Maybe, you could be the next co-chairman." Peter smiled. He was rewarded, seeing Toolah's eyes come alert. "I am not without certain influences," Peter said.

"Yeah–? Who, me? Mistress of *Chartreuse*?"

"Of course, Pearlee could--" Peter cleared his throat. "Well--recover the position." He gave the woman a meaningful look. "One might say, the position is within your grasp. You need only to 'seize the day.'" He chuckled. "Sorry. Inside humor."

Toolah did not catch the *humor*, but the meaning was clear enough. And she had intended to make certain that she, Toolah, would be crowned Grand Mistress. "That Pearlee won't recover."

Peter caught his body tensing. His intense anticipation greeted the woman's stillness--a gaze returned as frank insistence. He smiled a nervous bit of release, as he could only imagine what offset filter the woman employed, screening her immediate reality.

Her private thoughts she then revealed: "What better way, than to take away the one thing now dearest to her? That Regina is one to be satisfied. All know prissy missy Pearlee is straining their relationship. Fault Pearlee, 'cause--" The woman became highly animated, "she missed the mark! That Regina--? Good as got!"

...

Corey felt awkward soothing this woman who had been the stabilizing force within the group. But since the tragic loss of her dear friend Myrtle, the community had suffered. As sporadic as Pearlee's responses to the needs of her "family" had been, her generous purse strings was ever available. Things truly plummeted, however, after her love-mate abandoned her. Any could now no longer expect that private word of reassurance, or the much appreciated gentle touch of genuine concern.

"Pearlee, Regina has been gone for two weeks. Of course, you'll miss her." Corey added a timid embrace. But nothing reached this powerhouse of a woman. Local politics had always held a special interest for her. Yet, Corey learned that even the woman's own platform against abortion did not revive her.

It seemed all the more strange to Corey that he should be consoling Pearlee of a love interest that he had himself lost to the woman. But he understood pain--how it rips into the heart and burst wide the flood gates. Not only did he have to stand aside, the two women depriving him of connubial bliss; he himself had become an instrument of pain, discomfort for Mrs. Odum. During a selfish moment, he foolishly succumbed to the girlish whims of this matron. And now, she appeared to be completely disjointed. She would find every excuse to touch him, to telephone him at inappropriate hours, and to inquire of his whereabouts during his nonappearances at the *Chartreuse*. And when they were in each other's presence, this meeting seemed awkward, straining the atmosphere. And those renegade emotions--feelings of pain, confusion, regret—appeared to be as bars... maniacal imprisonment.

Aside from Pearlee's painful, debunking incident and love-mate loss, guilt, conscience caused Cory to relinquish the Lincoln; he was, therefore, again on foot. The long trek was not without the accompaniment of thoughts. It was being rumored that Toolah was the leading candidate for Grand Mistress. How unstable was Toolah? Perhaps, thought Corey, that it would be to his advantage to withdraw from all social gatherings. He noticed a hint of disaster on the horizons. A definite hint. But could he give up his membership entirely? He decided to let the next function make this all-important determination.

"If all's well, no final good-bye. Even so, a final look at what could have been deserves a final 'thank you.'"

He convinced himself that this was the appropriate action.

"The Maffick of all Maffick--" he added, "the coronation of the Grand Mistress. And Toolah is queen bee!" The feeling of his own failings returned. As try as he might, he failed to be acclimated, he thus counted *self* as loss to the conscience and coveted cloying surfeit of the club.

Yet the upcoming event was this very night. The whole affair was a ball of anticipated pomp, splendor, and impromptu! Would he become caught up in the festivities? Or would he, somehow, gear his way away from the differential? A contract, social or otherwise, must embrace the heart—*intrinsic matter*—and not just surface principle. It must not only confer a code of governing, but it must offer a fair exchange among all interested parties. Corey puzzled over his inability to become a part of the group—a group that appeared pastel and serene at the beginning but loomed, of a sudden, angular and hostile. Such was not represented in the contract. Such irregularities left the contract null and void. Then, the wall flashed in Corey's thought—at once pastel and angular, and again serene and agitating.

...

"You made it! Good! Peter wrestled Corey's hand and smiled. "I could have got someone to pick you up."

"Sorry. A little late."

"No problem."

"No, it's me. I gave up my ride. Well, the club's ride. Thought I had time enough, then some." Corey debated whether or not to tell him about his decision—that tonight's function will determine if he remains a member or quit the society entirely. But tonight's event was already underway and Toolah entered, sporting the tiara of the Grand Mistress. She boldly encroached, usurping attention, intent, and commandeered the host to a back alcove—beyond a mauve partition. The abandoned Corey assumed that the two had some last-minute details to solidify.

From where he observed, the whispered shouts of the two suggested bickering. But elsewhere the festive mood was contagious. Members and their visitors sashayed finery of royal envy. Although posted as a semi-formal affair, souls all were highly genteel and delightfully civil. Party favors and unique decor echoed the sentiment of frivolity. This might be reasoned as the failure to notice that the Grand Mistress commencement of the wand-- "stirring the mystique" –was behind schedule. Yet that tradition must be preceded by the *Love-Mate Step-Off*. And this moment of personal rededication was essential before the formal crowning.

It was at this point that Pearlee entered, and everybody became aware of the time. Her pearl tinted dress with its Asian collar influence choked the throat and fell away at the back, to underscore the small of the back. It hung mid calf, suspended above silken pumps--and was seemingly gathered up, as rays spinning from a xenolith broach. The whispers crouded and compounded with the name: *Versace. Versace.* And again--*Versace!*

The instant Pearlee's present was apparent, Regina rushed to her side. The younger woman's face had been overly made up, and she had quilted herself in long sleeves and extended skirts. Thus, if Corey was able to discern correctly, Pearlee could well have surmised the obvious. She was still expectantly compassionate; was she thus irate!

Her one deep love, thought Corey--bruised... battered.

It was to no one's surprise, this anger that mirrored in Pearlee's face. Nor were Corey and others surprised to witness Pearlee make her way to the alcove--just as the two, Toolah and Peter, emerged from the hall beyond, off from the alcove. These two came face to face with the enraged Pearlee. When Regina joined the three souls and attempted to dispel the potential for hostilities, she became the catalyst for adding fuel to a smoldering situation.

"Bitch!" Toolah lashed out verbally. "Don't you ever get enough?" This woman's stare intensified. "You whorish stray. I whip your ass and whip your ass. And you--!"

The woman threw a glowering look at Pearlee.

"I marked you. Got your spot. Got your bitch. There ain't nothing for you here!"

"That is a point to be taken." Peter Dugan interjected, sheepishly.

The verbal assaults brought others upon the scene. But before Corey or others could breach the distance, Pearlee had slapped Peter, who faltered back against the collapsible partition--serving to conceal paraphernalia. Both man and mode flopped to the floor.

Toolah responded by back-handing Pearlee. And Regina only succeeded in being pushed away.

Peter could taste blood in his mouth. His jaw was sore from the forceful slap, and his back ached from the fall. "I'm taking the bitch out!" he swore.

As he attempted to right himself, his hand fell against a tray of discarded silverware. He retrieved a stake knife. Vulgarish verve spewed as venom from Peter's lips, as

Pearlee and Toolah entangled selves, souls in combative fury.

"Kill her! Kill the bitch, Toolah!" Peter shouted.

The instance of hearing her name caught the woman's attention. And within the second he thrust the knife into Toolah's grasp! It was an act Corey was already too late in preventing. Though swift was his action, he could not suppress the moment. As in Peter's mind, he himself had reached the panicle of power. All would do his bidding. None Could refuse!

A second later Corey's fist slammed into the man's jaw! And Pearlee was a match for the disturbed Toolah. Despite knife in hand, Toolah failed to get the upper hand. Peter, meanwhile, decided. it would, in deed, be better to take matters in hand. Thus, he went "back to the well"--the tray--and armed himself with a Gansu ten-inch blade and threw himself into the fray!

"Bitch!" Peter Dugan brought his fist down with the giddy force of a madman!

Regina suddenly leapt. Her body struck and toppled the entwined combatants off their feet. Before Corey could confront the maelstrom, Regina lie still. The knife was embedded in her slight frame.

Pearlee's heart froze.... Shaken, she began to tremble uncontrollably, as the fallen Regina lay at the combatants' feet. But Toolah, blinded by hatred and jealousy, saw only a grieving figure of Pearlee. The visages of pain, horror did not register. Driven by a piqued fit of madness, Toolah's knife found it mark!

Only then did the madwoman take in the obvious. The outstretched hand of Pearlee grasping towards the fallen Regina. Then a howl, only equitable to the primal heart, tore from out the insane woman! Her eyes were fixed, her whole body jerked about! The madness of the woman canvassed the surroundings. The woman's eyes locked on Peter.

Immediately Peter repelled! The look of horrific fear flushed his face! The atavistic entity before him was no longer human... *commanding fear.*

"Don't--! Don't let her at me! She killed Myrtle! A-and... she'll kill me, too! She'll--"

Corey grasped the implications immediately, but was held back by hands from within the gathered party. And it was at this point that the apparently mad woman Toolah, with beast like urgency, sprang! With cartoon-like effect, she snapped his neck! She then recovered her tiera and crowned her head in stunned silence.

The night who's lost its moon was filled with screaming sirens and a confusion of winking lights. Corey made his way into the night air, thankful for the change of venue. Within, the police were collecting up evidence about the vicinity--and recording the fallen bodies of Regina, Pearlee, and Peter. Without, a gentle breeze revived the drained young man. A hand absently rubbed at the wrist of the other. He knew that Shannon would be released-- reconsideration of evidence. He also knew that he would find no solace within the club. Now, completely alone, he, however, felt a relief--a release of confusion, of fear--as though a wall had been leveled.

Suddenly, *"The Chartreuse wall!"*

It caught Corey with a sudden start. It was the wall's inscription:

"Because of you, What grander love can endure," the young man read. Then he realized that the moon was full and visible. It allowed him to witness the wall's long silhouette loomed against the darkness.

"Could it be as--as camouflage?" Corey wondered aloud.

It had been there all the time.

"*Modus vivendi*" He marveled!

The abeyance and the obtuse; the reserved and the rectified; the tonal and the torturous combated for dominance. Could they not coexists? Corcy did not have the answer--just thoughts of Pearlee and the dark, dusty miles ahead of him.

Let Lester Lipton Live A Little Longer–Ladies!

By
Mitchell Alexander Jackson

PART I

I was at my desk studying when mousy Lester hurried into the room, slammed the door shut then threw the bolt, next collapsed against the door, completely out of breath.

It seems I'm always in that corner lately. My grades are on the downhill slide, and it's an effort just to keep them from plummeting haphazardly unchecked. There's nothing cool about poor grades; the brothers don't know you, and the girls don't want to. So, lately I've been spending my evenings in the dunce corner–as usual. But things went from bad to– Well, I had to double my efforts at odd breaks in the day, trying to get it together. And though Lester is responsible, in a unique way, for my poor grades, I have only fondest regards for the little man.

Lester and I have been roommates. He was fresh from the University–"this college on the hill above Harlem." Now he was down South. I never did find out why. But soon enough we became roaming buddies–since second quarter of my freshman year, when he moved on campus. Since the beginning, Lester had always been a very quiet guy who kept to himself. He didn't seem to fit into any circle. Oh he was smart, a real brain. But he didn't have the looks to interest a blind girl on a foggy morning. His looks kept him on unequal terms with the world. I felt sorry for him.

Looking up from my boring studies, I anxiously waited, anticipating the interruption. The figure of Lester Bernard Lipton, breathing heavy against the door, finally drew up without a word. The poor guy had his troubles. He glanced over at me, then back at the bolted door–as though not knowing which way to turn. He had been so much alone most of his life that when be became popular, he didn't know how to handle the situation.

I only wished I had his troubles!

"That was close," Lester breathed. His teeth, like polished chrome sparkling in the sunlight, jutted out beyond his large fleshy lips.

How many now," I sighed.

"Fourteen."

"How did you manage that?"

Poor Lester swayed his stooped shoulders forward, dragging himself forward. He dropped upon the bed. "Oh–you know." His sad voice died away.

I nodded; I suppose I did. He had told me often enough.

My friend Lester sood a bit over five-three. To top it off, my home-boy was rail thin! If you can picture a stomp of a gate post–I used to say to describe buddy Lester to my folks–with a wide forehead, a narrow chin, and a nose out to here–then you got yourself a Polaroid of Lester. I'm not one to hold a mirror up to another when it comes to looks. We all got to make do with our birthday wrapping. Beyond that, Lester's nose had been broken three different times–all when he was to young to remember. So, for the life of me, I couldn't understand the logic behind his spontaneous popularity. But that sudden burst of "Rose of Sharon" had wilted his perfect honor student record.

Last quarter poor Lester had gotten a "B." English. And a "C" in American Government. Doesn't sound like a major upset. But to know Lester Bernard Lipton is to know that this was a "melt down" in the making. It was–his own word–a "catastrophe!" And though we had little to say to each other at the beginning of our rooming together, the little guy became more and more distraught and more and more dependent on my helping to get him through his popularity crises. You better know, we became close friends!

"Girls.... It was more of an expelling of pent up anxiety, if any thing.

"Why don't you just choose one and pin her?" I volunteered further, "The others would get the picture and fade out of the picture, eventually.

"Eventually should have been yesterday! Besides, you know I can't do that–" he sputtered.

"Yeah," I said. And this one thing I did know.

Mystery of mysteries. Why do people always want what they can't own?

Ever since the beginning of the "Girls get Lester Lipton" campaign two quarters back, Lester and I have been as close as Siamese twins. I became his "bodyguard" (–not that his body was subject to any undesirable attacks, by my standards, at least). I was more a public relations go-between, I suppose, and everything meant for Lester had to be cleared first by me.

During that time, I also bought a little black book. And all the names, addresses, and telephone numbers that were forced on the little, meek Lester, I readily recopied into my black book. I now owned three such books. But when my grades started slipping, and no amount of studying helped, I had to shut myself away and get down to brass tacks. Even so, I too, grooved on Bessie and Bach—needing to give a little to this way and that. This left Lester very much on his own. And my man was being swallowed whole!

And it was this Lester who slowly pulled himself up, and set up on the covers. "Andrew. You got to think of something."

His plea touched my heart—but my grades had a padlock on my day's wallet. The risk was too great.

"My head's too cluttered just now, Lester. This darn history, with Benjamin Franklin proclaiming to the Continental Congress, "Let George do it!' Thomas Jefferson uttering, "By God, let's do it!'—only remind me of my dad's comment when I phoned for a little extra change. 'The Dickens, you say!' At once historical and literary."

Lester merely groaned.

"Oh, I'll think of something. I promise. Just give me a little more time." Coyly I added, "You got a date tonight?"

"Yeah," was his dismal reply.

"What you got planned?"

"Oh, the pizza parlor. Then a movie."

I smiled to myself; old Lester must have a little Italian blood in hi veins: pizza, the third night this week, and it's only Wednesday!

The lucky girl?" I made an effort to keep a straight face as I watch Lester's expression go sour.

"Sheryn Stokley."

"Oh-hah!" I could no longer keep my eagerness in check. "So, you're going to the Relief!"

"Relief?"

"I'm sure you have a *Point, Lane* or something where you come from. With the Drifters it was *Under the Boardwalk*. Or maybe, *Up on the Roof*," I explained

"I see."

Here in Georgia, the same. And here, with Sheryn Stokey–? It was always Relief Bluff. She was that kind of date. "Sounds like you're going to take in the view at the Bluff," I said casually.

"Huh–?"

"Going all the way, this time?" I winked.

Lester's mouth flew wide. "You're being sarcastic, Andrew!"

I backed off. But Sheryn Stokey was a real hot number. All the brothers knew how eager she could be if the guy was to her liking; so I felt obligated to advise him further.

"Better watch yourself," I ventured. Or you won't be a virgin much longer."

"Now, come off that, Andrew!"

I continued to muse over the meekest of men's titillation predicament. It's astounding how girls throw themselves at this gentle mishap of nature. A Merrick he was not. Still looms that mystery–*why?* He's a sore sight, even if he is a brain. But what's really surprising is that he can carry his weight in conversations of any subject, on any level–but sex; in which case, he becomes as mute as a giraffe with laryngitis!

It seems that because he knows so little about sex in general, the girls feel glorified in teaching him. And with every lesson, he becomes more and more disgruntled. Only I knew his secret. He's a celibate! A strange existence for the human condition. Perhaps his religion prohibits sex of any sort. Of course, this is a guess on my part. Lester doesn't make a clear argument in this area. But what is clear is that female intuition has kicked in with just about every girl he's met. It's almost as if the girls suspect it.

A great failing of human nature is to desire the unattainable: whereas my friend, Lester, was impossible to reach, I was always readily agreeable. But there's no pleasing some women.

As I continued to gently mull over this strange dilemma during the stretch of silence, the logical response blossomed. "That's it!"

"What?" My disquieted friend came alert.

"You've been playing your cards all wrong," I said.

"I–I don't play cards."

"That's why you're getting your pants whipped off! Don't you get it? It's because you're a lousy card player. You're too transparent, Lester. Bet you never even heard of 'the bluff.'"

"I'm keeping my pants on, thank you," Lester returned, registering only to the more immediate of his concerns.

"And I'm going to help you do just that. Why with the old bluff and poker face, you can't miss."

For the first time in some while it seemed that his eyes held a look of hope. I responded to his gratitude.

"All you got to do," I guardedly replied, "is... take their pants off first."

"Now wait a minute–" he protested.

"First, hear me out. From the start, Lester, weren't they trying to get to you? It was you fighting them off. Well, right?"

Lester hesitantly nodded.

"Now, what if the situation were reversed? After all, there are two sides to a coin, the law of gravity, reverse polarity, and everything." I was groping to make a point. I guess it showed.

"What do you mean, Andrew?"

"If the girls love the side you show them," I said, "then show them the opposite side. If what you do give them a real high, do the opposite and bring them down to earth. Lester, if they back you into a corner with deliberate intentions, throw the switch. Man, make them back up over the same stretch you were obligated to cross. Just be the aggressor," I challenged him. "And they will automatically take up the defensive."

"Really?"

"My man, you can only go so far, and then they'll have to unhitch–say something like, 'Sorry, but I changed my mind.' A woman's prerogative, as they say."

Lester looked on questioningly. "What's to keep me from going all the–? You know."

I answered his uncertainty with a fact that could not escape him. I flatly asked. "Did you go all the way?"

"No, but–"

"So there! Nothing added nor detracted. The situation remains stable. The same... only reversed.

"Andrew, I am aware of the Chaos Theory. No, don't think so."

"Chaos Theory doesn't create chaos. It allows for the creation of the familiar, even during chaotic times."

"But whose familiarity, Andrew? Mine or the girl's? I mean, how often do so many girls find themselves competing for the same one guy? Who winds up getting *la vida de familiar*?

"Look, Lester," I said, sounding as positive as I could. "Trust me. The only change will be your switched identities."

"Reality."

"Okay, realities. In the beginning, the women were positive in their actions and you were negative in yours. Now you'll take up the positive role, thereby–" I pause for greater emphasis.

"The girls will be inclined to take on the only roll available to them. Not just a reality check, but a roll reversal!" Lester exclaimed.

"And I guaranty they won't like it one bit more than you do."

But the weight of what he must commit himself to–or perhaps the gravity of an undesired outcome must have struck home. "Or you sure–?"

"Proof positive! Try or die," I reminded him.

For certain I was far from sure. But I saw no sense in snatching away what little hope he had after I sweated nails driving that bit of hope into him.

"Well, okay. But you're coming with me."

"Huh-uh."

"I'll get you a girl," he persisted.

"Too much homework," I replied.

PART II

When 9 o'clock p.m. came about, Lester stood at the bedroom door, dressed in black ankle-boots and a gold color jump suit with black embroidery. "I can still get you that date if you're interested," his voice piped out anxiously.

I knew that he could, even at this late hour. But then, so could I. My little black books carried the same names and numbers as did his. I could make that same phone call. And all I had to say when the girl picked up was:

"Lester B. and I are double dating. Want to come along?" There would come a squeal through the receiver, followed by: "Lester B. is my sugar baby! Come on over!"

This time Lester was prepared for my response. "I'll be glad to help with your studies when we return," he said.

"Tempting." But I knew that I must not be persuaded.

The matter of my father's financial stance against my present grades, of course, was a factor. But I knew that if a draught of any kind were drank tonight, its crucible must not be tagged as having been influenced by me.

Lester stood poised for an explanation.

"You know my concentration is– Well," I said, "I'm no Langston Hughes. I lose a thought and it is gone. Not cut out to be the brain you are, Lester. No, you go. And remember–think positive. My man, make her cry uncle!"

He started towards the door then turned. "You sure?"

"Reverse identity. Can't miss! Displaying the greatest of confidence I added, "Now go get 'em tiger!"

Actually, I saw it as a fifty-fifty proposition: either he will or he won't!

In recapping Lester's peculiar predicament, I felt that if he did manage to become the aggressor and went beyond the point of no return–if he did go "all the way"–it would be only because that hot number of his encouraged that trip to the moon. Celibate or no, even Lester would have to say, "How sweet it is!" Furthermore, who's to say that Sheryn Stokley isn't the very "rib" of Lester. At any rate, I reminded myself, she could be the catalyst to bring old Lester to his senses. I mean, a little taste is no disgrace– when it's all said and done, I grinned. Besides, whoever of a religion that didn't encourage its followers to "be fruitful and multiply," right? After all, what survives without this one necessity?

I had already turned away as the dishearten Lester walked through the door to keep his rendevous. "The hot Sheryn Stokley," I heard myself say. Then I crossed my fingers. But for the life of me, I didn't know if it were crossing in honor of Lester's preservation—or initiation.

. . .

Barely drifted off to sleep after retreating from a stint of trig, I felt myself being drawn awake. Lester stood in the semi darkness.

"I did it!"

Was he grinning? My sluggish brain yawned... sparked. I grew alert: Good glory, man, it's about time! The thought raced through my head. And for once I felt a true bond with the now smiling Lester Bernard Lipton.

"Huh." I said, turning to stare at the clock on the bedside table—3:45 a.m. "Go—go to bed, man..." My body cried for sleep. And what's so revealing about lost innocence?

Five days later and the new man Lester was already at my desk when I walked in during a free period. But this new Lester was taking on the characteristics of the Lester of old.

"What's on your mind, Lester?"

Lester fidgeted with a button or two. It was almost as if he was trying not to look me in the eye. And I instantly knew that that little tryst of the other night with Sheryn Stokley was returning to haunt him. There was a "buzz" on campus. And between the snickering an finger pointing, I caught wind of an "Andrew" or two. And now he's come to lay the blame directly at my feet. So he was deflowered! And how am I to blame! I only offered moral support. If a guy can't be a buddy to a friend without being blamed for everything going wrong, then that friend is not a buddy! Who needs him! I held to this thought and dove in—feet first.

"And how did it go? Wednesday night and Sheryn, I mean." If he wanted to hang his life's dissatisfactions on me, then I would make it clear that I'm no longer providing a sympathetic ear.

He can think, *et tu Brutis,* or I can make it clear—very clear. I gave him an all-knowing wink.

Lester's mouth flew open.

A sudden melting of resolve? A feeling of betrayal? Whatever it was, I will end it pronto. After all, he did say that he did it. His doing! His responsibility! And there was no mistaking that grin of the other night.

I walked over to my bed, set upon it with regenerated peevish sentiment. I then encouraged my best friend: "Lester, give me the facts. Don't skimp on the details." There! I had inquired openly of what was the gossip of the whole campus—the seduction of Lester Bernard Lipton!

Lester dropped onto a chair. For a moment I thought I saw Lester catch his breath. "It—it happened. Just as you said it would."

"What?" My hopes fell hard with disappointment. "You're saying--"

"Everything went on as usual… in the beginning. And all during the pizza and through the entire movie."

Lester's pause left a gaping hole of reflection for me. Lester and the hot Sheryn Stokley. Finger pointing—nothing more. How much have I lost?

The little man continued. "That Sheryn kept throwing herself at me; it was enough to make a monk sworn to silence scream right out! I cajoled, coasted, quelled… Andrew. I did all but appease."

"Yeah, I'm beginning to believe," I replied.

"But I have faith in our friendship," he continued. "You're always there for me. So, when we were alone– Sheryn and I– You know, in her car at Relief Bluff, I took the initiative. She couldn't believe I was the same person! After holding her own in maintaining her honor, she started her car back towards the university. But I didn't let it end there."

"You–"

"I pressed the issue, eh, engagement. And--" His face brightened.

"You didn't--"

"You've always been a trusted friend. After all," he added, "only gentlemen stop when told. So, just for good measure, I became a real nuisance. And it paid off!"

Now his large strip of white glistened at this pronouncement.

"That Sheryn got so mad that she put me out of her car. Andrew, I had to walk the three miles back to the university."

During the unveiling of the details, I found myself with pent-up breath. Now, I all but collapsed back upon my elbows. I watched as little sparks danced in his eyes; it was undeniable that he was pleased with himself.

"A nuisance? That's what hot Sheryn Stokley called you?"

"The perfect nuisance, to be exact."

"But the finger pointing," I replied. The grapevine... gossip? The other snickering girls?" I had brought myself to ask the question, yet the answer was as obvious as three now little black books.

"Oh, you know."

The smile vanished. The little man seemed not so happy with himself. Well, who needs him.

"Word got around."

This new fain Lester returning the old, marked matter-of -factly. "The girls who were so eager to get something started is now something less than distant."

Although I tried to prepare myself for the inevitable. I still had trouble absorbing the knowledge of my great loss—and one step away from tossing my little black books out of the window... and Lester after them. I tried to assuage my feelings of loss with the frown I saw draw out across his face. His frown deepened, as I toyed with the thought that, maybe, he regretted his actions, now that he's no longer in demand. And I silently wished that he'd long remember and bemoan the good thing he had alienated.

"A nuisance?" Again the dreaded words fell from my lips as I looked at the image that had commanded every girl's dream. Now yesterday's pizza. How can I continue to be a friend to the likes of him? Sure, times had been good, as Elvis would say—girl crazy good. But when that mouse of a man cut his own throat, he cut mine as well. Hadn't I heard my name also whispered about? No, no friend would do a buddy that way. Sure I rode his coattail. His gain was my gain—and I made good use of it all. Just because he didn't have a taste for candy doesn't mean my sweet tooth should have to suffer. Oh, I'll get by. Maybe as usual. But having indulged in kingly delights, I can never again be satisfied with a peasant's palate. Lester's out of here!

"Well–" I began, and with the greatest of incentives to be cruel. "What's the matter? That's what you wanted, isn't it?"

"Yeah. I guess." He pulled on an oversized ear; his frown, if possible, deepened even more. "But now the department's typists and clerks are beginning to proposition me."

Amazement struck me hard across the face, and I almost fell over from the blow. It was so unexpected! "Like-like who?"

Lester took no notice of the shakiness in my voice. "Well, Mrs. Johnston. She's been broadly hinting for some time now. And there are others."

"You mean, the Mrs. Madam la madam Johnston? The divorcee?" I –wide eyed could utter no more.

"Uh-Huh. And–"

"Wait a minute," I croaked, "what–how?" S

"Well, word got out that I was all action. Too hot to handle–even for hot Sheryn Stokley."

I grinned, "I guess that would do it."

"Any way, she said that she can handle me just fine. It was bad enough with the young ladies," he moaned despairingly. "But now–I mean, those older women can be murder."

"Yeah." Now grinning from ear to ear, I said, "You're in the big leagues, now! Wow!"

"Andrew," he pleaded, "you've go to help me. Please think of something."

I could feel our friendship growing by the minute! How could I refuse him with this new predicament he found himself in? If anybody knows Lester B. Lipton, it's me. This was too heavy a burden for him to shoulder alone.

I cleared my throat. In a tone reminiscent of the Rudy Vallies of olden days, I filled the moment with my presence. "Let me worry about this," I said.

Lester sighed. Very relieved, he left to make a two o'clock class.

To have thought the thought about the poor little guy! I chided myself, but good. I was, perhaps, the only close friend he had. And he was, in deed, my very dear friend. I'll have to think of something, I assured myself—with the warmest of smiles—and made a mental note to purchase three more little black address books. Never can tell how long it might take.

THE FAIRY WHO STOLE MY CHRISTMAS WISH

By
Mitchell Alexander Jackson

In Bold Daylight
Part One

"Now, you don't believe in Hallowe'en goblins, ghosts... or even *Santa Claus*, so I don't expect you to believe in imps or--fairies. That's why I'm hesitant in telling you about–well..." the old man cleared his throat. He sighed, then lifted his chest and leaned forward in his chair and whispered–"the fairy who stole my Christmas wish."

Next the old man fingered his beard that hung white over the greater part of his chest, alert to any response I might give. I gave none. He settled back in his chair... relaxing, somewhat–but said nothing.

Has it been seven years? Still, here I find myself–doing little more than "patchwork." I had grown wise to the ways of these senior citizens–or rather, the "forest of wisdom" had pounced upon me much like the forest of *Barnum Woods* upon *Macbeth*. I now knew that their "confiding" in me was their way of usurping attention. For instance, Mrs. Johnston had once made me her accomplice in getting the entire Sinclaire police department and half the town to camp outside her modest home in the belief that she was being held captive by two previously escaped criminals. And then, there was Thomas Stanley who led me to believe that his shoplifting spree was an illness on his part. But, after my continuously pleading to various shopkeepers in his behalf, I later learned that shoplifting was his queer form of entertainment. Therefore, have I since learned to just lean back in this swivel chair of mine and "toy" with my ballpoint pen. As now... I wait–wise to the ways of these oldsters.

"See here," and the bearded man reached into his shirt pocket and produced a small, worn address book, flipped several pages, then laid the red book open on my desk. "See that?"

A small, pressed leaf lay stiff on a blank, yellowed page.

"A clover," I said–not sure what I was to make of it.

"Not just any clover, young man! A four-leaf clover. Count the leaves!"

"I can see that. But, what does it suppose to mean?"

"My wish, of course!" He said. "The wish that fairy stole from me!"

"But the clover–four-leaf clover," I corrected myself, "is for luck, isn't it? Or did I, as a lad, cheat myself of all the wishes I may have held with every clover?"

"Did you have a horseshoe and, say, a shiny, new penny?"

"No." I said cooly. "But isn't a horseshoe worth three wishes in itself?"

"Umm– Yeah." The old man fluffed his beard. "You get three wishes, but you can't depend on them. I remember one Thanksgiving–we were kind o' poor, you see–and I had this horseshoe.

So three times I wished for the family a chicken. We got three turkeys! I hate turkey! No, no," he said adamantly. "Just can't depend no them. And with inflation these days, it's best to have a clover and a shiny new penny to go with that horseshoe. Then, young man," he thumped emphatically, "you can be sure of one wish, at least.

I raised a brow slightly, though not the least surprised; for I was merely becoming impatient. Still, I'm paid to listen, if little more, so I said, "Mr. Winterpegg, what do you want from me? Want me to do–?

"Your help. I want you to change my luck. They stole my wish, and I want it back."

"They?" I said.

Oh, I didn't tell you. There were two of them. That fairy had an elf with her. And the two of them went and stole my wish."

"And how did they *steal* your wish?" I asked pretentiously, "Did you make a wish, then changed your mind, and so, used the wish without receiving it?"

"No, I was tricked!"

"How?" I was becoming exasperated.

"I dreamt it."

"Beg pardon?"

"When I want to sleep, young man. One must sleep. I dreamt my wish. And well–they peered into my dream. Yes, you heard right. The impish elf entered my dream as that fairy reject appeared at my bedside. Devious she was!"

"Meaning?"

"Chanted some words over me as I slept. Then that– that elf fellow ripped my dream away. And–in horror–I cried out: 'No, no! No!' Awoke and saw the two of them– laughing. Dancing! Round and round my bed–and sing:

"'The wish *you* would wish on *Christmas Eve*

"'Is no longer yours... but *ours* to perceive.

"In an instant, I lunged at the little thieves. But they winked out. *Nothing.* And I landed on the floors. Don't know how long I laid there, but when I opened my eyes, there she was. Her flowing ball gown sparkling... a rainbow of colors. Another fairy she was... and floating just above me. She lifted me to my bed with the touch of her wand. No wit bigger than the first. Only three feet tall. A certainty. As the rogue looked more a child, this fairy seemed the perfection o' maturity–and ladylike.

"A *Promise* fairy, she said she was. And she told me how I can get my wish back. But I'm an old man; I'll need help. I've thought on it and thought on it. Decided on you–because you listen"–and then, as though some revelation: "To hurdle a wall, one must first address it. Don't you agree, young man?"

"If I am to help you–eh, find your wish, you'll have to tell me what your wish is." One obstacle at a time, I thought.

"But if I do that, it might not come true. No–can't take that chance."

"Then, what–"

"Well..." He brushed his white beard aside and reached again into his pocket. "I've here," and he placed the items on my desk as he said, "a pin, a piece o' bacon, and a shiny, new penny."

I studied the items briefly: an ordinary straight pin wedged in a strip of corrugated board, a fatty piece of bacon, and a brand new penny. I ventured, "So–?

"So, Mr., eh–Josh." Clearing his throat, he pressed on. "First, sir, we have the pin. I prick my forefinger... here. Put a drop o' blood on this page. Then I prick yours, and your blood is added to mine. Well, like... so." The deed was done before I could mount much of a protest. "Next," he went on, "this penny is placed over that spot of red, and... then the piece of bacon here over that."

"What effect can this have on–" I broke off to nurse my wound.

"On regaining my wish?" Mr. Winterpegg added: "Oh ye of *little* faith." He shook his head, "But now, we turn the page," he said and did just that, placing the four-leaf clover upon the page. "So," Mr. Winterpegg breathed reassured. "We now close the book, and maybe– Do you have a rubber band?

I fished into my desk, produced one. "Uh, would green do?"

"Fine! Fine!" The old gentleman beamed. And after he finished binding the little book, he addressed me with an air of sternness. "This book must be kept in a safe place. But I am an old man–with dreams, and they would be able to find it through my dreams. But you, unfortunate man, yet the stalwart youth... shoring up the walls o' practicality. You know such demands as hopes and dreams. No. Your hopes aren't based on *wishes*. You can not dream. So, on your bleak... empty nights o' sleep, this book will keep safe. And on *Christmas Eve*, my wish will come true."

"Well, Mr. Winterpegg." The scolding had left me feeling less than hospitable. But patience is a necessity when dealing with this crowd. "True," I said. "My luck isn't based on hunches. And dreams–? I consider them a falsehood–waste of energy that could be better used towards a more constructive period. It's obvious we're not on the same wavelength. So, what makes you think I'll go along with it all?"

I was somewhat surprised to see the old man grin–just a little. Then he said, "Because you listen. What you hear you may not like, but–because *I believe* in them, you'll respect my beliefs.

And that's more than the person who doesn't listen would ever consider doing. You will hear me out."

135

I became intrigued, feeling almost appreciated. "And how would I know if anything becomes of this?"

"That you won't look foolish when it's over–? 'Tis a pity you exercise so little faith." The old man thought a while. Then he said, "What if I were to show you my wish on Christmas Eve?"

He *show* me a wish? This I had not expected. He can't tell me his wish, but he will show it to me. I was shaken with skepticism, yet intrigued. "Uh– And where–?"

"Here," he said, reaching the small red book towards me. "Just–" He fanned a hand about in small circles, absentmindedly. Just write your greatest desire in the book."

"My–?"

"Greatest desire."

Then I had heard correctly. "And this will show me what you wished for?" I asked, doubtfully.

"But of course! However, at the *proper* time." His reply carried a smile. Warm, perhaps genuine. "Go ahead, young man. Don't be shy about it," he said, as little lights danced in his eyes.

The thought just *flashed* in my head–right then and there. Still I don't know why I did it, unless subconsciously I was striking back after the many abuses suffered at the whims of these senior citizens. So, with mischievous intent, I removed the rubber band. And the miniature tome lay open before me. I settled on the next available leaf–the page immediately following the clover. I then wrote: *Will You Marry Me....*

That should throw a monkeywrench into the works, I thought, as I confidently replaced the band around the book. Let him make whatever he could of that!

Mr. Winterpegg triumphantly got to his feet as I reached the address book back to him. "No, no." Then he mused, "Oh, I see I've forgotten a matter of much importance." He reclaimed his chair. Hesitating, he gruffed his beard, then commenced anew. "In order to make the whole thing work, you must place the book in—say—a *Christmas* stocking one minute before twelve midnight... on *Christmas Eve*," he added, with the raise of a brow. "Just a moment before *Christmas*, mind you."

Before I could construct an argument, he, with the most gracious of carriage, eased his small, bulky form from the chair and through the doorway.

At the closing of the day, I could scarcely prod my weary body from behind my desk. The little address book given me... for safekeeping—*that peculiar Mr. Winterpegg*—I picked up and slid into my breast pocket; I checked the contents of my valise, then started out for my apartment house. It had been a long day.

. . .

Two days had gone by, but I saw nothing further of Mr. Winterpegg. And as peculiar as that group of senior citizens appeared, Mr. Wintrpegg was truly *"sui generis"*—peculiarly unique. Now, the striking of an old grandfather clock down the hall woke me from slumber, as usual. And as usual—I toiletted, breakfasted, and went to the office. Most unusual, however—the strangest of things... the items in the drawers of my desk seemed pampered with. Of a certainty. And pen... desk calendar were not in their proper places. Still, I attributed it to the whims of a busy-body superintendent. The following block of days ensued without further incident: "A place for everything and everything in its place"–"God's in His heaven, and all's right with the world," *et cetera, et cetera*.

Come three days before Christmas... the office limited activities to the morning hours. At twelve noon, I boarded the public transit for Combelbee and Sterling. This was my first opportunity to see Sterling in all its holiday splendor. The strings of holly transversed the length of main street, draping very available cable and lamp fixture. Candy canes, bells of red and white and green, even *Santa* and stockings aligned the street–with each store hailing its own special greeting.

Hoards of busy shoppers bustled about.

On completing my Christmas shopping, my parcel tucked under my arm, I was hailed by my lady friend, Miss Gladys Rampart. "Josh! Joshua! I see that you finally got time to do your Christmas shoppng." She had a mountain of packages, all wrapped and ribboned. After spotting small, flat package under my arm, she remarked with the zeal of the holidays: "And who is the lucky girl?"

"Oh. Some young lady I've been seeing for a good while now."

"You know," she said, "I've been seeing a certain guy for several years, and he's given me a head scarf and matching handkerchief each Christmas. You wouldn't be giving your girl a like gift, would you?" She asked, eyeing my package suspiciously.

"Now, that's for her to know," I jokingly chided. "Need any help–?"

"I thought you'd never ask!"

"Well, I know how stand-offish a woman with some independence can be," I volunteered.

"I'm referring to hands-on volunteering. Mister, talk is cheap." She winked.

. . .

Fatigued from our excursion into "window-shopping", I was more than happy to curl up in bed for an early night's slumber. And when the old clock woke me the day before *Christmas Eve* I had imagined seeing the strangest little individual peering from the foot of my bed. With high cheek bones and wearing green, bibbed pantaloons that fell short at the calves, he appeared to whispering to some other I could not see. Then in a wink, he was gone. I rushed to record what I imagined I had heard. With pen and paper I wrote down the sounds and peculiar syllables; they made no sense.

Later, at the office I puzzled over the unintelligible script for a little part of the morning. And after completing a nourishing brunch at the Inn House, I telephoned Gladys. She suggested that I accompany her in doing some "last minute" shopping. It was during this task that she told me of an unusual, yet humorous, tale that left me somewhat uneasy.

It appears that a great-great grandfather, who had been freezing to death from a harsh Maine winter, was rescued when the to-be great-great grandmother fitted him into several pairs of her long flannels. The old gentleman considered this a form of engagement, apparently—for they were married soon after. Now it seems it had become a "family tradition" that when a Rampart female was sure of her man but couldn't get him to the altar, *she* would make the proposal, or at least a hardy suggestion, by presenting him with a pair of flannels on some special occasion.

I gave a nervous laugh at its close. And all the rest of our touring, I could only offer up nervous smiles—and hope that Gladys did not notice the uneasiness there. I'm sure Gladys knows that I will propose at the proper time. And, of course, she isn't the kind of woman who'll result to trickery. She knows me better than that.

The thought maligned my spirit to the point that dear Gladys urged me to take an early leave. With reluctance, I left her side to shut myself away for the rest of the evening. Still, its presence had the occasion to linger. That thought—collectively expressed in the "patrician" and the "feminine"—disordered me. And it kept me tossing... the whole of the night. 'Tis ever a wonder

sleep found me....

But... As Goes Night
Part Two

Comes day....

Christmas Eve burst forth with the ringing of carols throughout. Church bells tolled spiritedly of the season, and everywhere could be heard the expectations—of adult and child alike. Late shoppers hurried about with parcels overflowing. Merrymakers crowded the lanes and broadways. And *"Santas,"* in their bright red on street corners, called out in merry "Ho-ho's!"—as their ringing bells tolled of the fate of the less fortunate.

There was no escaping the holiday spirit.

Soon I, too, burst forth—with a spirited chorus of "Jingle Bells." Such is how Gladys came upon me. And she went as far as to tease that I was commencing upon my second childhood.

"I'm amazed," chimed Gladys. "You were never the emotional type! That wall of yours is crumbling.

This bit of reference to a "wall" startled me somewhat; for it alluded to an earlier statement made by the elderly gentleman, Mr. Winterpegg. However, still caught up in the holiday mood, I merely hinted, "Birds of a feather...."

Gladys linked her arm in mine and blew a kiss up at me. I pretended to catch it on the jaw. "Forever," she whispered.

Unlike myself, who had been an only child–and an orphan fending for himself since his fourteenth birthday– Gladys is from a huge family with strong family ties. All the aunts, uncles, nieces, nephews... and an assortment of cousins... return from all corners of creation for a mass *familiar–en masse.* As Gladys' fiancé –informally, of course–I am always invited to her family's *Christmas Eve* gathering. For whatever the reason, I had always "begged off." Apologies accepted. But this *Eve*–at Gladys' insistence–I called on her at seven o'clock in the evening... in casual attire.

The early arrivals were busily preparing for those yet to arrive. And hopefully only Gladys noticed my presently agitated state. After introductions and a minimum of courteous exchanges, Gladys–ever *simpatico*–spirited me out into the gardens. We nestled upon a mauve, metallic swing. She interlaced her fingers with my own.

"You responded better than I had hoped," she mused. "At least you didn't lose your voice completely."

"Attribute it to the miraculous wonders of the holiday spirit," I replied.

Her head had been cradled in my chest. But Gladys then looked at me with a bewildering smile and raised brow. "You're not one to speak of miracles, let alone spirits! Could it be that my family has got you sprung at wits end–?"

"It's just that I'm not accustom to mob gatherings," I offered.

"Oh, you–!"

Of course, I began to laugh. And so did she.

"I love you," said Gladys, inclining her head towards mine.

Truly, I'm far from the romantic cut, for I later learned that I had fallen asleep in but the turning of an hourglass.

When I awoke, a candy-striped pillow was under my head. And except for the glowing lights of the house and gardens, the surroundings were in darkness. My Gladys stepped out of the shadows with a look of puzzlement. "I'm sorry about falling asleep," I ceded.

"Oh, if I wanted a *Casanova*, I'd have snooted when I saw you coming." The Gladys offered up a belated smile.

"I'm not sure how I should receive that," I replied, somewhat puzzled. "Gladys–is there–is there something wrong?"

"Oh, no! No, umh. No. It's probably the lighting playing tricks on my eyes–I suppose. I've had a fairly tiring day... as one can imagine. And well–what with lodging and dining preparations.... You know, I can appreciate a quick nap about now."

We two reclaimed the swing. Gladys glided a caress upon my forehead. I offered her my shoulder.

"I shall do my part, to be sure," I ventured.

"You're quite a bargain, after all.

"But no *Casanova?*"

"Much better," Gladys broached. "Umm-uh. You're the security a woman needs–even when her needs are secured. Especially so when... half convinced she is seeing little green men."

I sprang to my feet. "Little green men!"

"Oh, Im sure it must be fatigue. What imaginings...! And if they hadn't appeared so frightfully real, I would be enjoying a robust laugh just now."

"How many were they," I coaxed.

"As well as I could make out—two. I suppose.... And I don't suppose they were actually green; it must have been the lighting. But then— If it were so, they couldn't have been real. Oh, Josh! Wha-what's happening to me—?"

I did my best to comfort her. "The commingling of lights and shadows in darkness does have a way of stimulating the imagination. But as a dream—locked away in the human subconscious—there can come revelation. If you're up to it, dear, please—continue."

"Well, if it's really just a dream, what does it matter if they had been green," Gladys said with confidence. Still... what was most peculiar was that sing-song speech of their."

I volunteered: "A chant of some kind, maybe?"

"Yes. Oh, like—" I could almost see Gladys' synaptic bridging, as she said: "Why, yes! Like English spoken backwards.

"What?" I reached into my wallet and took out the coded piece of paper from the night of my strange dream. And it became all too clear.

"All the while dancing about you. Uh—chanting rhyme," dear Gladys said. "Next I heard you murmur something back to them."

"Oh, no!" I cried.

"What's the matter?" Gladys asked. Concerned.

"That bell— What does it mean?"

"Oh, that's just to summons every available person to decorate the tree and put out the presents."

"I—I got to go," I said.

"Of course, we will."

"No, I mean, I must leave. What time is it?"

"Fifteen 'til," said Gladys.

"'Til–?"

"Twelve, she returned. "Why?"

I placed a hurried kiss on her cheek, then dashed for the gardens exit. Any explanations much come later. I could hear her light footsteps echoing from behind me. But I dared not stop. For time was quickly slipping away.

The grave urgency of time pressed heavily as I reached my apartment house, unlocked the broad, weathered door leading from the streets, and raced up the long, narrow stairway. On reaching the second floor, I stole a glance at the old grandfather clock at the top of the landing–five 'til twelve. I wheeled about, and at full stride I reached the door of my quarters, only to remember having left my chain with key into the door to the street.

Without hesitation, I stepped back, then rammed a perfectly good shoulder against a perfectly stubborn door. As I sat crumpled on the floor of the hall, enduring the pain of a battered shoulder, I heard the light, quick tapping on the stairs. Gladys appeared. She rushed to my aid, and apparently to my delivery.

"Josh! Why are you on the floor! What's happening?"

"What time is it?" I pleaded, "Time.... The time!"

"Oh, Josh, really!" Gladys said as she stooped to help me to my feet.

"No, dear, I must get in. I–"

"Then you shouldn't go leaving your keys about," Gladys chided. And she managed to fix the appropriate key into the door and turn the lock. She pushed the door wide then froze. The room was in tornadic disorder. And in the midst of the upheaval stood two little, green figures.

In a dash I was after the two rummaging thieves. An imp had just claimed the little, red book and tossed it to his accomplice. I made a grab for her, but she winked out into nothing–tossing the book back to her companion as she did so. And to their satisfaction, I jounced between them, over sleeping cot, upon chair, into cabinet–tripping and falling, but never, never letting up.

Dear Gladys, bless her heart, "snapped to" just as I thought I would fold from exhaustion. And the two of us tackled both simultaneously. The imp tossed the book to the child-like fairy and winked out. Suddenly, my "dare-devil" Gladys made an impossible spin on her heels and leapt into space, to snatch the address book from plain air.

"I've got it! I've got it!" She bounced upon the little cot, waving high her victorious gain. The imp and a sneak attack sobered her. Gladys managed to toss the little– and somehow precious–tome to me. Suddenly, the old grandfather clock down the hall started to strike the hour. And I knew that it was then too late. Time had run out. Still, I refused to give in. I "raced" over to where the ill-matched stockings hung. Truly, the *Apostle* would have approved! Next, I rammed the book down the smaller of the two–my being a little heady, possibly. The last of the clock's chorus died away.

All was quiet. *Stone* quiet.

The room was in shambles.

Gladys nonplus by the episode and out of breath: "They just–*vanished*." And then, as though remembering something long forgotten, she asked, "What is all this about, anyway?" She settled on the cot.

I espied the red and green head scarf and handkerchief set trodden underfoot. "I'm sorry, dear. I had hoped–"

Gladys stood, pecked me on the cheek. "Merry Christmas," she said.

In silence, I gathered up her present and dropped in on the cot–brooding over the racked affair.

Our stroll back to the Ramparts' was a little less than pleasant. In stead, my thoughts idled elsewhere.... During the days following the session with Mr. Winterpegg I had grown to think of *Christmas* as a special kind of holiday. And I'd half expected... and had wholly hoped to see the old gentleman the minute *Christmas* commenced.

Gladys was aware of my downcast mood. And the dear fretted so about my well-being that she chanced to place my dismal countenance in the heart of her family's *mass* of good cheer: "Can you stay awhile? The mob will be opening presents just now. And I do want to give you yours."

Any amount of resistance on my part seemed to fuel her insistence. And in the end, I breathed a sigh of resignation, as I stood amongst the cheery members of the largest family to ever I witnessed! An aunt or, possibly, a cousin was expressing her thanks, as she displayed her gifts before the approving relatives. She was followed by another family member, and that member by yet another... and another and.... The unwrapping of presents transpired the whole–the festive *heart* and *hearts!*

Finally, Gladys, in turn, reached beneath the huge, ornamented tree and retrieved a colorful package. "I hope you like it"

Gladys had directed her words to me. I made a modest protest. After all, her gift from me had been trodden underfoot.

"Shusssh...!" She said, silencing me with one tender finger against my lips.

The inevitable thus—be it must.

With hands suited for other matters and heart suggestive of affairs I know not what, I undid the delicate wrapping, then opened the box. Within that box—flat and wide—Its meaning clearly exposed: a colorful pair of long flannels! I was slain—discombobulated. My mind kept running the script: *underwear... red, flannel underwear*—over and over.

Eyes grew wide and a murmur rose from that sea of faces. Gladys' intent of marriage was clear. And now that army of relations knew. *Knew.* Every eye fell upon me. Gladys patiently waited. Am I to prove true—show all that she had done well in choosing me? I suddenly felt as though I was being suffocated. And speech took flight. I was unable to utter a word. Not word one!

The joy in my dearest's eyes died away. Mirrored on her face was pain—the pain that stabbed deep into her heart; the pain I had placed there... with nothing being said. My loving Gladys... sad, sadly turned away—to flee. Her home, her family was largesse enough to drown her sorrow. I—the outsider, the alone one—I headed towards the door.

But then there came the knock. An aunt somebody-or-other hurried off to answer the door and soon returned with a large box, her arms barely encircling it. "Why, Gladys! It's for you!" She exclaimed.

"From whom—?" The tearful Gladys appeared truly puzzled.

I'll never win her back now, I thought. A secret *amour.*

"Strange," the aunt replied. "But when I answered the door, there was nobody there. Just this stupendous, gloriously colorful box in the doorway. And I've looked, Gladys, dear, but there's no sender listed."

The "buzz" about the room grew even more loudly. And on the face of each and all shown wonderment. I now felt more alone than ever.

When my darling Gladys received the box, she announce with surprise: "Why, it not much heavier than a feather!"

The "buzz" exploded into "oooh's."

Gladys eyed me, with love teeming joyously in her eyes. She was so certain that I had sent the box–that I would never let her down. She set the box down and unwrapped it. "Oh! But there's a box within a box," she cried out.

All the more intrigued grew the "buzzing" body.

Gladys, soon having the second box undone–stuffing abound–found within it yet another wrapped box; a roar went up and cheers resounded about the room.

This presentation continued on, as I dumbly counted the disclosures. And with this smaller box, about a sixteenth the size of the first, numbered six. And this revealed yet another! With all spread about wonder and rumor, this smallest of the boxes contained the–the fruitage: a velvet-like box small enough to rest sweetly in palm of a lady's delicate hand. When Gladys opened this, tears flowed. She made no attempt to wipe them away. In that instant, I saw more love in her eyes than I had seen in all my thirty-two years of living.

"Oh, Josh!" my dear-heart cried. She threw her arms around my neck, "I will! Oh, I will, she sang.

The others shared her jubilation. And the women passed the small, velveteen box amongst themselves. I managed a glimpse of the bands–the rings–sparkling in the affective atmosphere.

Having my Gladys in my embrace felt good! But I knew that I had lost the right to make any claim to her–that, sooner or later, her anonymous admirer make his presence known. That I should be so irresponsible as to take advantage of her faith in me just now would only cause her grief. She would later despise me when the sender of the gift is finally revealed to her. And though I must lose her, I could not have her think ill of me.

Regretfully, I pulled away....

"Gladys–" My world was crumbling before me. But I had to go on. "My dearest, I–I'm not responsible. That–"

"What?"

Before Gladys could say another word, I charged forward. All had to be now: *love* and let her go... or maintain and be *disdained*. "I– I did not send the gift," I said.

Gladys just smiled up at me as though she had heard a bit of *Marvell* humor. "Oh, no?" She said, "Well, *mister practical joker,* even I can read your handwriting by now. And she showed me the small, yellowed page. It read:

Will You Marry Me....

"Mr. Winterpegg!" I cried out.

"What did you say?" My Gladys asked, somewhat puzzled.

"Oh," I thought... knowing that she would never believe the truth. "What a winter, eh?" I said, "I mean, what a winter to remember."

And then, my loving Gladys came again into my arms– as "the family" stopped admiring the ring set long enough to admire the two of us.

Said Gladys, "A *Christmas*, in deed. Your *P.S.* asserts... let me see: *Amor vincit omnia*. My Latin's a little rusty, darling. But, yes. *Love conquers all!*"

"I couldn't wish for anything better," I said—as she hinted at the overhanging mistletoe. Then, we drew close—kissed... long... and tenderly. And, of course, the cheers went up and lasted until... the end—and beyond.

SONG

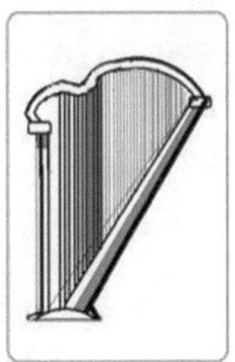

Ain't Just Razzmatazz

Oct. 23, 2007

INTRO:

You girls out there— [Spoken]
Are you asking yourself... [Spoken]

VERSE 1:

Whatever happened to
    The Lover man?
Who can do it like
    A rubber band?
    —Get you spinning like hot
    Chilli can?

Well, here I am!
I'm that loving man!

VERSE 2:

And, girls, you're never left feeling
    Without.
I'm gonna keep you, girl,
    In a shout
    —Get you spinning—'til you
    Shout it out!

Oh! Yeah, baby!
You're my loving man!

VERSE 3:

Baby, and know ...ain't just
    Honky-tonk,
'Cause, babe, I'm willing to
    Pack my trunk.
    —Get you spinning a cry:
    My sweet hunk!

You're so pleasing!
You're my loving man!

CHORUS:

No woman should
    Go her day
Without some special play...
And, girls—
    I'm here to say
    —This is your lucky day:
    This ain't just
    Razzmatazz,
    I'm into flavored sass!
    ---You girls!
    Sweet sassafras!
    —Lucky me!

ALL'S ALRIGHT

VERSE 1

There are three things
My *dear-heart* loves—
This blessing
The very Heavens applause.
Her three things
She pleasures most of:
    Black coffee
    Black Caddie
    —And me.

Three things
My *dear-heart* craves—
Whose love wings,
Satisfies in waves!
Her three things
She waits on for days:
    Black coffee
    Black Cattie
    —And me.

BRIDE 1

Don't you know that the girl's got it on?
Believe me—she ain't waiting long:

The coffee's black-black
And the Caddie's smack!
—And with me behind the wheel
 We do no wrong!

CHORUS (1):

All's alright!
All's alright!

My baby got me for her
Pure delight!
—From broad of day
To the stroke of midnight
All's alright.
All's alright!
All's alright!

VERSE 2:

Dinner... dancing—
My love and me:
Romancing
Is on the fly and caprice!
But, three things,
Her pleasures, you see:
 Black coffee
 Black Cattie
 —And me.

Squeezes
And late nightcap!
French *and* wink!
Then ever the tap!
Her three things
She craves pass the rap:
    Black coffee
    Black Cattie
    —And me.

BRIDE 2:

Don't you know that she still got it on?
Her smile says I'm not wanting long:
    The coffee's black-black
    And the Caddie's smack!
    —And with me behind the wheel
        We do no wrong!

CHORUS (2):

All's alright!
All's alright!

My baby got me for her
Pure delight!
—To broad of day
From the stroke of midnight
All's alright.
All's alright!
All's alright!

BLUES ME HIGH

Oct. 17, 2007

VERSE 1:

I had never seen a light
Like the lightning in the sky
    Blues me high.
    Blues me high.

Strike me gent'ly, like a lamb.
Spike loads of honey jam.
    Great supply.
    Great supply.

CHORUS (1):

Then you came along.
Everything went wrong:
    No blues the high
    Could not honey-jam that great supply.

    You smile, and I don't know why....
    Oh— what am I to do?

So, I'm floating in a dream,
And nothing's what it seems.
    Lean and shy.
    Lean and shy.

VERSE 2:

Well, I'm searching heaven high
For my own just heart's reply:
    Where and *why*?
    Blues me high.

No light out there—to be seen
Are dark clouds like a screen.
    Strain the sky.
    Strain the sky.

CHORUS (2):

Now my life is gray
Ills just ricochet:
    No answered "why."
    Instead, it is just a dark, dark ride.

    You smile, and I don't know why....
    Oh— what am I to do?

So, my mind is all now screened.
Sands of time are now mean!
    Bring me down.
    Bring me down.

VERSE 3:

  Other ways need not be   (There needn't be some
     found   other,)

As your guidance's more   (You can provide another)
   than sound
Light to life.   (Light to life.)
Light my life!   (Light my life!)

Give me just your warm sweetness
Returning completeness:
   Fire me twice.
   Melt the ice.

CHORUS (3):

Be my everything.
Make this soul take wing:
   Light the sky
   You can take me to that perfect high!

   You smile, and I don't know why....
   Oh— what am I to do?

So, do speak and smile—bubble
Hope into this rubble!
   Sift my life.
   Blues me high.

CODA:

Please---
Now, maybe, just your sweetness....
Return me to completeness:
    Blues me high.
    Blues me high.

GIRL

INTRO:

Even the Bole weevil was caught on the square.
Best turn the page to a love held dear;
But that *midnight special...*
Seams to visit... everywhere. [Spoken]

VERSE 1:

It never comes up
In conversation
(But) I only want a *normal* relation.
   You done me wrong
   Girl—
   I ain't that strong.

Girl!
You know that a man
On best behavior,
He only wants the *feminine* favor.
   Girl,
   Who could know
   That you're female poor.

CHORUS:

Girl!

Stacked so fine
And feels just right!
Girl, you are a soul's delight!

You steer me to the stars.
—But now I don't know
Who you really are.

How could you do it, baby?
Your feminine wiles
Just drive me crazy!
(How) I try to be your gentleman.
But, naturally, you ain't no lady.

VERSE 2:

Friends give a hoot
In recognition;
They laugh: You want *primeval* sensation!
    If womanly,
    "Girl"
    Pleases, they say.

Girl

I feel ridiculed
With only "flavor"
I'll never want your "special" favors
    I ain't that strong
    Girl—
    I'm moving on!

CHORUS:

Girl!

    Stacked so fine
    And feels just right!
    Girl, you are a soul's delight!

    You steer me to the stars.
    —But now I don't know
    Who you really are.

Your scent, your smile
Just drive me wild!
But—
Girl, it ain't my style.

So, tell me—
How can I be your man, baby?
—When you ain't even a lady!

Naturally [Spoken—in a whisper]

HAUNTING BROWN EYES

Oct. 15, 2007

CHORUS:

Oh—

Those big brown eyes,
Like rainfall from the skies!
Drowning out the pain... [Simulate the slow falling of
    raindrops]
And still drive a man insane.

How
Do I hide
A heart now hypnotized?
Hide this longing heart
From those big brown eyes!

VERSE 1:

Mister, tell me--- [This line spoken]
    I know you got a train
    Headed somewhere.
    Drifted up—just up from Abilene.

    Crossing the *Great Plains*
    Don't even compare
    To the greatest love that I have ever seen.

Done crossed the *Great Divide*;
And *Mason Dixie*;
And rambled along the old *Mississip'*.

But I just can't hide
From what haunts me—
Just can't give those haunting eyes the slip....

[CHORUS sung here—second time]

VERSE 2:

Okay, so let it rain.
Let the sun blaze.
What life's got to offer, I don't mind:

Smiles... or drowning pain
For all of my days;
But not those big brown eyes—all the time!

She says that she still waits—
Waiting for me,
'Cause there's more to life than lose or win.

My heart takes the "bait,"
And it begs me.
But something 'bout life won't let me give in.

[CHORUS sung here—third time]

CODA:

So, tell me---

Mister, got a train
Headed somewhere?
Drifted up---just up from Abilene.
I'm haunted—near insane
—Help me stay clear
Of the greatest love that I have ever seen. [fade out.]

HE WAS HER HERO TODAY

Oct. 12, 2007

VERSE 1:

It was just another war
One he wasn't looking for.
Bowing out would of been okay;
Yet, he went any way.

It was not the bureaucrat
Out there watching his back
—With their *shortages... a* shame!
Yet, still he made a name.

BRIDGE:

...And so turns the world of blood,
Confiscating her one and only love.

CHORUS:
He was a hero today.
Yes, he saved many lives.
Great was his sacrifice:
He was *her* hero who died.

　　Now she's a love-heart torn
　　With sweet memories unborn.

Left to a world of score,
It's now her heartbreak alone.

VERSE 2:

Friends gave their condolences.
Their consoling made her wince:
Here, *their* loved ones all free from harm;
Herself could spew a storm!

Her loss: grief upon a tide.
Her life ended when he died;
They act as if life goes on;
Her hopes, love, dreams—all shorn!

[BRIDGE sung here—second time]

[CHORUS sung here—second time]

VERSE 3:
And the steps are slow and paced.
Yet seams all so out of place.
Drum beats the solemn toll all round.
—She feels half-buried now.

And the honors are not spared;
Her heart missing *sweet times* shared
Caused the laurels to go unheard
As her thoughts cried the words....

BRIDGE (2):

...And so turns this world of blood,
Confiscating my one and only love.

CHORUS (2):

He is a hero today.
Oh— he saved many lives.
Great is his sacrifice:
He is *my* hero who died.

    Now I'm a love-heart torn
    With sweet memories unborn.

Left to a world of score,
It is my heartbreak alone.
CODA:
Yes...
[Sing the Chorus and fade out....]

IT'S ALL DOWNTOWN

Oct. 17, 2007

VERSE 1:

I feel the steel
  In my eyes.
I fee the spark
  Realized.
  —Can't do much but listen.
  And not so much about that.

Upon a time
  I could see.
Upon a time
  We were free
  —Dreams and schemes at being,
  And so, sporting in the Black!

CHORUS:

I could not see
  Nor believe—it's real.
I never thought
  What was wrought
  Would ignore the way I feel.

How could this be?
  On the eve—to heal,

The future wrought
   Vicious thought
To reduce... all life repealed.

Now---

   It's all *downtown*.
   Is the whole world turned upside down?
   Yes, it's all *downtown*.
Can it ever be turned around!

VERSE 2:

I know "what for."
   It ain't good.
I know the score:
   Heart of wood
   —And so ticks the turning,
   All in a fever-like bortsch! (All in a fever-like pitch!)

Yesterday's done.
   Like a breeze.
Yesterday spun
   Future seas
   —How so cruel's the turning
   Cloaked ticks... backward Tudor torch! (Clock-ticks...
backward Tudor hitch!)

[CHORUS sung here—second time]

LIVING IN THE BLUES, BABY

Oct. 14, 2007

BRIDGE :

Oh, Im...

Living in the blues... now, people.
It's all blues living—both night and day.
Stuck here in old Hot-Lanta:
Like a hard, hard woman, she done sucked my joy away.

VERSE 1:

Should of listened to that woman
Should of listened when she said it's time I go.
Her bed's now hot and steamy
With every other Johnnie... and some come-lately Joe.

On my way to the station
That old Greyhound is gonna bay me on off
Grateful for those tire paws;
Let her come to know my leaving's gonna be her loss!

CHORUS:

She's got'em
Coming from the North!
Clam-happy in the South!

173

—I talk until I'm hoarse
While she's burning down the house!

No more Hot-Lanta, people.
I'm getting the hot hell out!

VERSE 2:

Recall, baby, that old saying:
There's a great many fish in those seven seas!
New line bought I now, woman!
Gonna test every water---casting off your yoked
    miseries!

[CHORUS sung here—second time]

BRIDGE:

No, more...

Living in the blues... now, people.
It's no blues living—both night and day.
Stuck here in old Hot-Lanta:
With a hard, hard woman, who done sucked your joy
    away.

VERSE 3:

Giving up these blues, woman.
Ain't, woman, gonna live these blues for you no more!
Keep your Hot-Lanta, baby
—With your Johnnies and your Joes! 'Cause I'm long
    out the door!

CODA:

Woman! [Spoken]
You know you done me wrong! [Spoken]

I'm getting the hot hell out! [Sung]

Living in the blues.... [sung. The last word is held for a
    very long period, until it dies out.]

LOOKING FOR THE MAILMAN

Oct. 12, 2007

VERSE 1:

Looking for the mailman [mumm-humm!]
Got a good woman.
Got me a good woman
Out there in Sheridan

Moved up there from Cheyenne;
I used to live in Sundance
So—
Mailman hurry her letter
Straight to me.

—You see....

Met her in Jackson Hole
—Heart and mind *was* closed.
And how that good woman
Really touched my soul.

Oh!
Betwixt the cold and the snow
I took a chance
And found romance
So—
Mailman hurry her letter
On to me.

[CHORUS sung here—first time.]

VERSE 2:

Looking for the mailman. [mumm-humm!]
Letter from Wyoming.
Just like the Cheshire cat,
See me sporting a grin.

"Packing" for romancing.
Boots now buffed for dancing
So—
Mailman hurry her letter
Straight to me.

—You see...

Giving up the rodeo.
Circuit working no more.
Got my own sweet filly:
One fine circumstance!

Oh,
My sights are ready, you know:
Hair-lined romance
Giving her a chance
So—
Mailman hurry her letter
On to me.

[CHORUS sung here—second time.]

VERSE 3:

Looking for the mailman. [mumm-humm!]
New path a trailing
Gonna tie that *love* knot;
Keep her with a warm fire.

Steeped up in desire.
She and my heart conspire.
So—
Mailman hurry her letter
Straight to me.

Gonna start the family:
"Little feet" agree.
Living sweet on the life,
Touching heart to heart.

Oh,
No, it don't take much art—
Just commitment,
'Cause she's heaven sent
So—
Mailman hurry her letter
On to me.

[CHORUS sung here—third time.]

CODA:

Now I'm free!
Free to love again, my friend.
—Sweet life...
For her and me!

So,
I'm looking for the mail man.
Yeah.
—Just looking for the mailman.
[Pause]
Looking for the mailman!!!

CHORUS:

—*Don't you know* [Spoken]

It was blazing trail, my friend.
That door to romance just opened
     Up again:

A heart overgrown—memories of thorns
     Just ended.

In that Western pass
     A love that would last found me
     Wrapped about me.

My poor heart revived
     And *old* memories...
     Just died.

LOVE'S SMILE

Oct. 14, 2007

VERSE 1:

Don't be smiling at me
Like you're my granddaughter.
No more looking at me
Like you're my granddaughter.

I never knew your momma.
Or her momma, too.
Or those sometime "uncles"
That her momma approved!

No, no, no, no, no,
No, no, no, no, no, no---

VERSE 2:

Don't be looking at me
Like some lose granddaughter.
No more smiling at me
Like you're my granddaughter.

I never knew your momma
—So, there can be no past.
Contend me this old shack;
I'm fixed as the crabgrass!

Yo—

CHORUS (1):

Go you way, girl!
No more to say, girl!
—No payback. No loss love.
Life's tough, is all!

Once upon a time
I was without a dime.
—Your folk chose... less to love.
Life is tough, is all!

So—

VERSE 3:

Don't be smiling at me.
Go seek out another.
No more smiling at me.
Girl—don't even bother.

Consider not my bankbook.
—No spying under my bed.
Got myself a bank-box.
It's ensured by the Fed!

No, no, no, no, no,
No, no, no, no, no, no—

VERSE 4:

Don't be smiling at me
Girl, you're no granddaughter.
No more looking at me.
Her momma knew another.

I never knew your father
Or your "uncles," too.
Or those "aunts" that clustered,
Raising hell and roof!

Yo—

CHORUS (1):

Go you way, girl!
No more to say, girl!
—No payback. No loss love.
Life's tough, is all!

Once upon a time
I was without a dime.
—Your folk chose... less to love.
Life is tough, is all!

So—

VERSE 5:

Don't be smiling at me
— Never knew your grandmother
No more looking at me:
I'm just the one who loved her.

That woman was my heart, girl,
When your mother was new.
But she toyed with my heart, so:
Tore it straight in two!

VERSE 6:

Now you're smiling at me
Like some loss granddaughter
No more looking at me
—Look just so like your mother.

I never knew your momma.
Or her momma, too,
Who preferred the "uncles."
She was never true!

No, no, no, no, no,
No, no, no, no, no, no---

CHORUS (2):

Go you way, girl!
No more to say, girl!
—No payback. No loss love.
Life's tough, is all!

If you wish—then stay;
It's said, love makes a way.
—You so chose... me to love.
Love is grand, is all!

So—

CODA:

Now you're smiling at me
Like you're my granddaughter.
Girl, you're looking at me
Like a loving granddaughter...!

Yeah, yeah, yeah, yeah, yeah,
Yeah, yeah, yeah, yeah, yeah, yeah!

Like a loving granddaughter...! [Fade out —in
    repetition]

No Heart's Ease

Oct. 14, 2007

VERSE 1:

...And I die
A little longer
Living lesser... every day.

And I cry
Out my hunger
With no lesser... prayer to pray.

   And no word.
   And no heart's ease:
      Just to live on... in desperate play
      —By every
      Tome, Dick, and Harry
      —Peter and Paul!

CHORUS:

On my knees—I continue to pray.
My knees—bowed... through night and day!
And the world—whole world spins about.
Alone—and... all is locked out!

On my knees—
I continue—on my knees!

VERSE 2:

Now I see
A little closer
Feeling lesser—every day.

As I tire
Of the plunder
With no lesser—prayer to pray.
   Still, no word.
   And no heart's ease.
      Just *give* and *take*... and *take away!*
      ----By every
      Tom, Dick, and Harry
      ----Peter, and Paul!

[CHORUS---sung here second time]

CODA:

On our knees—I continue....
On our knees—still I pray
On our knees—we continue.
On our knees—bowed night and day.
On our knees—and the whole world....
On our knees—spins and bouts!
On our knees—still oppressed souls...
On our knees—alone... locked out!

On our knees—I continue.... [Fade out ---with
   repetition.]

Nothing But Trouble

Oct 11, 2007

CHORUS:

Nothing but trouble.
Nothing but trouble!

When the river rise,
Know the dam must bust.
When you're despised
And low on trust—

Tick-tick... Tick-tick... Tick-tick... Tick-tick.... ["tick-
    tick" represents the drumming of time.]

   Ain't nothing but trouble....

VERSE 1:

With the passing of the storm,
All bathed in sunny calm.
And the *waters:* less than ankle deep.

A chopper hovered overhead,
Just as a child's soul was fed—
While carpeting down a greenly hill of sleet!

[CHORUS sung here—second time]

VERSE 2:

And the nation voiced all 'round,
And breathed a sigh of down—
As slumber spills from the waking eye.

No great devastation seen;
Feared expectations—lean.
This Katrina bullet, all thought, passed them by.

[CHORUS sung here—third time]

Begin waters then to fuel
Impressions—weird, surreal—
With the giving way of the old dam.
And the "Lady of beads and mirth"
Was she next called up a hearse:
And was this precious lady thus overwhelmed.

[CHORUS sung here—fourth time]

CODA:

Nothing but trouble....
Tick-tick... Tick-tick... Tick-tick... Tick-tick.... ["tick-tick" represents the drumming of time.]
—Trouble!!!

ONCE WE WERE LOVERS

Oct. 23, 2007

VERSE 1:

Half expect to hear
Your knocking at my door,
While my heart
Hungers for
That something more.
   Absently,
   I look beyond
   The window glass
     —Absently beyond...
    And into the past.

BRIDGE:

We once
Were lovers
Once were we true:
   Were once
   The hopes and dreams
   Of each the other knew.

VERSE 2:

...The repast.

Yesterday it seemed
Your loving touch did say:
With this heart,
Love, always—
I pledge to stay."
   Lovingly
   Your smile caressed
   The wine-filled glass
     —Lovingly beyond...
     And into the past.

[BRIDGE sung here—second time]

...But, alas.

VERSE 3:

And, so, now—a lone
I'm pacing 'cross my floor.
All my heart
Yeaning for
That love once more!
   Helplessly
   I look beyond
   The window glass

—Helplessly beyond...
And into the past.

[BRIDGE sung here—third time]

CODA:

Yes---
We once were lovers...
Once were we true.... [Fade out]

ONLY IN HARM'S WAY

INTRO:

One red head—my friend said---
Is all you need today.
One red, one blond ain't no alarm
—Just keeps you in harm's way!

VERSE 1:

Here, all my cares
With growing new fears
Keep me taking it on the chin.
Then, a friend
This time
Caught my state of mind.
He was sporting the broadest grin.

VERSE 2:
Now, his glad-rags
Well, they weren't half bad.
My own, though, a cut above his.
"In the biz?"
Ask he.
"No, just the melee,"
I said, "of the corporate frizz."

BRIDGE:

Smug and trim
I matched him grin for grin.
"How goes it," I said to my friend.
Without a pause of the natural laws
He smiled:
"Just short of heaven...."

CHORUS:

One blond
One red head, is what he said,
Is all you need today.
One red
One blond ain't no alarm---
I'm only in harm's way.

One blond
And one red
Will make your day
—You're only in harm's way.

VERSE 3:

Well, now ten years
And corporate wares
Keep me taking it on the chin.
Like a sin
That shines

Preying on the mind
Always is his great big grin!

VERSE 4:

So, I go bold
This one day and sold
Off that cooperate way of life.
Kind of nice—
All free.
Just my ax and me.
Just a grooving—not thinking twice. (Grooving on—
    an *not* thinking twice!)

BRIDGE:

Smug and trim
I matched him grin for grin.
How goes it? I'll tell you, my friend.
And with no pause of the natural laws
I smile:
"Just short of heaven...."

CODA:

One blond
One red head, is what I say,
Is all you need today.
One red

One blond ain't no alarm---
I'm only in harm's way.

Yeah---
One red head—my friend said---
Is all you need today.
One red, one blond ain't no alarm
—Just keeps me in harm's way!

PICKING SOME POSIES

Oct. 12, 2007

INTRO:

Life is a stage, we say.
And every one must play their parts;
Each trading golden dreams.
In return: broken hearts!

VERSE 1:

Life's often "come-what-may"
And every one must play a roll
—From dawn to broad of day,
On through dark, dark night.

Lonely souls pass this way
Loving hearts all—grown cold
As nothing calls... to stay:
Too soon is lost delight.

So—

CHORUS: [sung here—first: "I'm"]

I'm picking some posies
For a real gone girl.
She left me for another
—And I'm stuck in her world.

Just thinking on roses
For a loss love true
...Is only Hollywood romance
...Is only Hollywood romance
It's only Hollywood romance!
   Can I start a new?

VERSE 2:

When first comes love along
The gladden heart now smiles at play
The world now smiles in song
Life feels all so right!

Soon, too, is joy next torn
And no thing is okay.
All hearts are ripped on thorns
—Too soon is lost delight!

Oh—

CHORUS: [sung here—second: "he's"]
He's picking some posies
For a real gone girl.
She left him for another
—And he's stuck in her world.

Just thinking on roses
For a loss love true
...Is only Hollywood romance
...Is only Hollywood romance
It's only Hollywood romance!
    Can he start a new?

VERSE 3:

You may be just that one
And being denied your true love
—Another love to come
Sparks your life... and light!

Carom! Your world's undone
—Losing new love anew:
A pained heart to be shunned;
Pitched into dark, dark night!

So—

CHORUS: [sung here—third: "she's"]
She's picking some posies
She's a real gone girl.
He left her for another
—And she's stuck in his world.

Just thinking on roses
For a loss love true

...Is only Hollywood romance
...Is only Hollywood romance
It's only Hollywood romance!
   Can she start a new?

REMEMBERING OUR LOVE

Oct. 23, 2007

VERSE 1:

...And I wish to say
I do love you still
—Even though
  We're in late December.

We started out in May
Embracing ringed wills
—As before
  Our love has know no bounds.
CHORUS:

Remembering our love,
Revisiting the time
Is now no less a joy of need
Than an endearing wine.

One sweet embrace—and all!
Two souls—one mind
Love cherished now—as then!
  —As though the first time....

VERSE 2:

And recall the way
You so sweetly smiled
At the door
Of my heart—remember?

The sun and stars displayed
Dreamings every mile
---Down life's road
    Our love has known no bounds.

[CHORUS sung here—second time]

VERSE 3:

And, now, let me say:
I do love you still
—Even though
    We're in late December.

Now, hand in hand, may
we embrace ringed wills—
Kiss. And so—
    Our love has known no bounds!

CODA:

Love cherished now—as then!
Love cherished for all times!

SHOO-SHOOING

Oct. 19, 2007

INTRO:

Shoo-shoo, shoo, shooing
Shoo, shoo-shooing
—Moving on down the line....

VERSE 1:

Baby, I'm [Spoken]

Shoo, shoo-shooing the blues
Making notice of her crime.
Pitching all the rubble
And any kind of trouble in kind.
'Cause that gone woman
Ain't no woman of mine!

Let me say [Spoken]

Living just the blues
Because of that woman
Catch me in the blues night and day.
But, baby, if you're giving,
I won't be turning any away!

So, rock me!
—If you get me.
Come and make a liar out of me.

Turn it on! Turn it Up!
Baby, turn it every way, but free!

    Shoo-shoo, shooing.
    Shoo-shoo, shooing.
    Turn on the rocking!
    No need for stopping.
    If you're giving, baby,
    Let's get to living!

    No need for stopping.
    Keep up the rocking!
      Shoo-shooing, baby.
      —Moving on down the line!
I'm [Spoken]

Shoo, shoo-shooing doldrums—
Breaking bottles of the wine.
Breaking now the web hold:
That woman spun her weaving so fine!
Now, that gone woman
Ain't no woman of mine!

That's why I say [Spoken]

Living no more blues
Because of that woman;
I live for each day this time.
So, baby, if you're giving,
Come be that sweet, sweet lady of mine!

Let me hear it, people! [Spoken]

CODA:

[Same as Intro—but repeat and fade out]

Shoo-shoo, shoo, shooing
Shoo, shoo-shooing
—Moving on down the line....

THIS HOLIDAY CHEER

--Oct. 11, 2007

INTRO:
   [Strike the lower "G" key once.]
People–
The past ain't always in the past....
And holidays never last. [Spoken --- first three lines.]
   [Strike the "E" key three times to *echo* "Jingle Bells!"
   Repeat a second time.]

[Yeah]
This season, they say, is for
   Merry-making.
For me, it's all just
   Reflection.

Glad tidings
   Are ringing--
A season in keeping...

   –But
   Old sorrows
   My bottle's nursing....

They curry the night
   With cheerful delight–
Morning breaking!
   Still, merry-making!

...And year afer year
   For me, just my tears....
Sadness to the bone—
   Left out... alone.

It's the season!
   Me---without you!
   The season.

VERSE 1:

Oh—

How is it true—
   Is it you, baby?
I didn't think a body
   Would remember.

Only a few
   Stick like glue, baby.
So, nobody ever
   Calls this number.

   Another holiday *chimes* round
   And nobody's ringing my bell.

CHORUS:

...And so the *bells* ring
[...And, yes, the *bells* ring] *[Read from Second verse as
   first line of Chorus]*

And I'm without *love*
In my life— not a new thing:
I lost at the dice.

Call it a crime!
—So hard, sometimes.
Bells ring out for lovers,
    Not for me.

It's a merry, merry Christmas
    Time of year.
    —Here
I'm wrapped in misery....

VERSE 2:

Oh—

Was yesterday
    A-okay, baby?
It's been a while and so I
    Can't remember.

Well, you can guess
    Life's a mess, baby.
And so nobody ever
    Calls this number.

    Another holiday *rings* round
    And nobody's ringing my bell.

[CHORUS –sung]

VERSE 3:

So—

You're living well,
   I hear tell, baby.
Doing more than alright's
   Late December.
Now, here you call.
   I feel small, baby.
Love's own one true body
   I took under.

   Another holiday *tolls* round
   And you, baby---ringing my bell.

CODA:

[Yeah]
This season, they say, is for
   Merry-making.
For me, it's all been
   Reflection.

Glad tidings
   Are ringing--
A season in keeping...

–And
Old sorrows
Got my heart bursting....

They curry the night
   With cheerful delight–
Morning breaking!
   Still, merry-making!
...And year afer year
   For me, just my tears....
Sadness to the bone–
   Now, not... alone.

It's the season!
   Me—and with you!
   The season.

'Cause
Another holiday
Rolls round...

And baby, [spoken]
Here you are [Spoken]
Ringing my bell!

[strike the "E" not three times to echo "Jingle Bells."
   Repeat a second time.]

TREASURY OF LOVE

Oct. 19, 2007

VERSE 1:

Let it rain.
Must it pour.
Let soon the pain—at my door
    Weep like the panes
    There in my window:
    —Drumming refrains
    As the winds blow.

CHORUS:

And it's all
Because...
I know no other soul
Who brings forgetfulness
    —With hope of a new-found bliss!

    To slay me—oh!
    Elevate me so!
    And heaven ward—
    It feels so good!
    Enraptured!
    With a kiss!

All my heart to hold;
Treasury of love
Tenfold.

VERSE 2:

Will I then
Feel release.
Weeps rain... a friend---bringing ease.
   Escaping then
   —No tear stained pillow
   Drumming refrains
      As the winds blow.

[CHORUS: sung here—second time]

VERSE 3:

And my dream?
Gone—long pass.
She'd been my queen—nothing last.
   Reaping no gains
   While on my pillow.
      Weeping refrains
      As the winds blow!

[CHORUS: sung here—third time]

CODA:

All my heart to hold;
Treasury of love.
Unlike the panes
There in my window:
—Drumming refrains
As the winds blow.

WITHOUT HER IS NO LOVE

Que pasa?

CHORUS:

What's the matter, baby—
Are you still sitting lonely?
What's the matter, baby...
Did you lose your one and only?

Oh—
Your tears are a heartbreak!
And I can see you are a lady
—Who made that one mistake....
Let me help you nurse the heartache!

VERSE 1:

Old times and lost memories
Surface now and then:
    Steer me to the nearest bar
    —To nurse the beer and gin.

Every day much like a breeze,
Until she walked in:
    My world came crashing down
        —In a tear!
        Her standing there so near!

[CHORUS sung here—second time]

VERSE 2:

Loves are known to go and come
In the thralls of time:
    First they make the heart to sing,
    —And then to blow the mind.

And so, I thought love was done
Oh, but---she was fine!
    Sat Poised —and in silence
    —and alone...!
    My heart now not its own!

[CHORUS sung here—third time]

BRIDGE:

Oh, people–

What is life, now,
Without her...

You must know the way
I love her...

    Will only make me pay and pay
    ---Should she ever go and stray!

VERSE 3:

New love, at Cupid's urging,
Led me to her side:
    I pulled up the nearest chair
    —My fears I could not hide.

And so, she nodded, caring
—Two tears touched her eyes:
    My world being reborn---
    Cupid's hug.
    She touched my heart in love!

[CHORUS sung here—fourth time]

VERSE 4:

Two hearts dancing 'cross the floor
Bridge the lonely years
With more dreams of happiness
—Now, no more silent tears.
And so, aspirations soar
—Two hearts sharing cares
    And our love is stronger
       —Even still.
       Love binding hearts and will!

CODA:

No more worries, baby—
No more sitting lonely.

No more worries, baby!
'Cause I found my one and only!

Oh---

No tears and no heartbreak!
And still the perfect lady.
You snatched my life from fate.
—Together no more heartache!

Winkings Of My
Sweet Gladys

—Elvis Aaron Presley—

Oct. 18, 2007

INTRO:

Come, my Gladys—come to me
   —Be my love.
Be my love, my sweet Gladys...
   —Set me free.

VERSE 1:

As the time rolls on
And I grow alone
And the year piles on and on
I look back to see
The old memory
Of a heart that wished would be:

   Sweet touch every night
   Sweet dreams delight!
     —Arms wrapped up in arms.

CHORUS:

Well—

Heard about *Alice Cooper*

—The *fuss* of the ancient past;
   But my whole soul
   Is growing old
   Thinking about my Gladys!

Once was I young and hardy
When *cuss* colored the young lad.
   Was my whole soul
   Still longing for
   Winkings from my sweet Gladys!

VERSE 2:

But the "now" is here,
And my heart is there,
And I find no peace no where.
And my one love sweet
I could never meet;
Now, my heart is in retreat.
   Sweet love every night
   Sweet touch delight!
      —Tears without the wares.

[CHORUS sung here—Only its second half]

VERSE 3:

And, so, love is lost;
"Heartbreak" is the cost.
Yet my soul will not grow false.

How I "burn" and weep.
How I long for *sleep*.
In the arms I could not keep:
   Sweet dreams every night
   Sweet tears delight!
      — Love and heart betrothed!

[CHORUS: sung here—Only its second half]

[CODA: same as Intro]

Song: Winkings Of My Sweet Gladys
Author: Mitchell A. Jackson
Created: Aug. 16, 2006
Artist: Elvis Aaron Presley
His female persona: *Gladys*
   ---5:30 p.m. local news account.
Definition: *Elvis*
El = god
vis = a) force*; power
vis = b) visible, visual*
   —Could it be that Elvis was bi-sexual?
   * Represents the writer's definition preference.

WOODEN ELEPHANT

1972

INTRO:

Mama-san and a cup of rice
Silk and lace—huh, huh. No dice.
Drugs are too costly a sacrifice
—And I ain't comin' over to this place twice.
'Til I get what I came for, I won't go.
You know what I came here for—

BRIDGE 1:

   I came for my large wooden elephant
Of Southeast Asia
I crossed the seas to be here.
I came for my large wooden elephant.
And I ain't gonna leave 'til I get her.

BRIDGE 2:
Left your ho-o-o-ome.
Right!
Left your fri-e-e-ends.
Right!
Left your gir-r-r-rl.
Left the outside world!

My ho-o-ome!
Left.
My fri-e-ends!
Left.
My gir-r-rl!
Left.

Left.
   Right!
Left.
   Right!
Left, soldier. Left.

VERSE:
There's a war goin' on right over the hil-il
Left, soldier. Left.
Where blood of foe and friend bein' spil-iled
Left, soldier. Left.
And I be there to foot the bil-il
Left, soldier. Left.
'Cause it's my duty if not my wil-il
   Be it right
   Or be it wrong
   I take with me my thought in song

BRIDGE 3:

Left.
   Right!
Left.
   Right!
Left, soldier. Left.

CHORUS:
   Sol-dier march o-on
   Supply the glory to your own say sto-ry.
   Sol-dier march o-on
   —And ride the heavens rollin' high!

Great Mighty's Will

1973

VERSE 1:

Oh, the leaves in the trees begin to show.
And the sun--yes, it comes out once more.
But, oh, my love... oh, where did you go.
Well, I guess
It's the Great Mighty's will.

VERSE 2:

Oh, the wind gently blows through all the trees
And the plants--they have sprung from little seeds.
And, oh, my love... I beg please, please, please!
This and more
--If the Great Mighty's will

VERSE 3:

Like the bees make their honey, I'll stick around.
And the wasp build their nest, I'll settle down.
And, my love, we'll start off on even grown.
Yes, my love,
--If The Great Mighty's will.

CHORUS:

Starting now, and forever––
Starting now, I will never
Out my heart have you stay.
You will always
Be with me
In my heart--of each day....

SPECIAL NOTE: All Songs Were Created By Mitchell
Alexander Jackson.